WISDOM
TO KNOW
THE
DIFFERENCE

Sujata Ives, PhD

Your Work, Life, & Success Guru

©2025 Sujata Ives, PhD
Wisdom to Know the Difference
eBook ISBN: 978-1-965761-49-6
Paperback ISBN: 978-1-965761-50-2
Hardcover ISBN: 978-1-965761-62-5
Ingram Spark ISBN: 978-1-965761-51-9
Library of Congress Control Number: 2025912036

Editor: Dr. Jeannine Bennett, PhD
Cover Design: M.A. Rehman
Interior Design: Marigold2k
Publisher: Spotlight Publishing House™

www.drsujataives.com

WISDOM
TO KNOW
THE
DIFFERENCE

Sujata Ives, PhD

Your Work, Life, & Success Guru

SPOTLIGHT
PUBLISHING HOUSE

Goodyear AZ

Dedication

Dear family, friends, and colleagues,

I am deeply grateful for your unwavering support and love; you have enabled me to live a life filled with purpose, meaning, and perspicacity.

Much Love for Rob, Raven, Bryten, Evan, Jeff, Leight, Mary, Pam, and Wade.

I could not function without our doggies: Khaleesi, Orion, and Broonie!

I extend my heartfelt gratitude to the NCDA, APCDA, MCDA, World Council for Intercultural & Global Competence, UNESCO, GIC, ACA, MCA, and NSA where professionals, colleagues, and mentors have welcomed and valued me.

Without you, I would not have the courage to be who I am.

I love you all!

Sujata

In your soul are infinitely precious things
that cannot be taken from you.
~Oscar Wilde~

Introduction

Authoring a book on wisdom serves several meaningful purposes, and there are many reasons why I wanted to write such a book during times of uncertainty where discontinuity was the only constant variable. I want to help you turn the extraordinary power that your perception reveals into wisdom, and your wisdom into **perspicacity**.

Leaders did not know what to do through the world pandemic. Nor did they know what to do to restore the "new normal". They failed to consider wisdom. I am asking leaders to consider that there are too many wars, conflicts, disputes, disagreements, clashes, tensions, and differences. We need the power of wisdom now!

I truly believe that the first responsibility of a great leader is to define reality, through wisdom, for everyone.

Preserve and Share Hard-Earned Wisdom: Wisdom often comes from experience, reflection, and the synthesis of knowledge over time. I go further than synthesis and want to say that it takes something I call "**Knowledge-Sifting**." There is so much information that's coming at you like pouring rain that you have to take the time to sift through all the noise. Write down the really good pearls of wisdom.

We are drowning in information and starving for wisdom.

Offer Wisdom in Complexity: In an era of information overload and misinformation, people do not only need facts, but they also need perspectives. Wisdom helps others make sound decisions, understand nuance, and navigate life's uncertainties. And you can definitely feel the uncertainty in the air these days.

Promote Self-Awareness and Growth: A book on wisdom can serve as a mirror, prompting people to reflect on their values, behavior, and long-term purpose rather than just short-term goals. Wisdom can also take people out of their ignorance.

Counteract Superficial Thinking: Many modern narratives focus on quick success, external validation, or instant gratification. A wisdom-centered book encourages depth, patience, and meaningful living. I know that you can delay gratification. You have been given the power of Free Will.

Bridge Generational and Cultural Gaps: Wisdom often transcends time and place. This book can serve as a vessel to reflect on truths and universal principles in a world of constant change, noise, and information overload.

Perspicacity is the quality of having a keen sense, insight, common sense, and discernment.

Perspicacity (or perspicaciousness) is defined as an acute discernment (from the Latin perspicācitās, meaning thought sightedness, acumen)—a clarity of vision or intellect that provides a deep understanding and insight. {Google Dictionary}

This highlights wisdom, intelligence, and insightful, sound judgment. What I specifically call "**Perspicacious Intelligence**".

Perspicacity is the ability to perceive and understand things quickly and accurately.

This requires insightful thinking, mental acuity, and the capacity to perceive subtle details often missed. That is the intelligence part!

It is frequently linked to individuals possessing mental acuity, observation skills, and the capacity for sound judgment based on insightful understanding.

In a job description from the Journal of Science, NASA published an article in 1966 titled, "Scientist Astronauts: Only the Perspicacious Need Apply." The astronaut recruitment efforts summed up perspicacity in this way:

*"The quality most needed by a scientist-astronaut is **"perspicacity**. He must be able to quickly pick out, from among thousands of things he sees, those that are significant, and to synthesize observations, develop, and test working hypotheses."*

This job description can be applicable to many others.

Does your job require you to be able to quickly pick out, from thousands of things, those that are significant so as to integrate observations, develop, and implement?

I call this "Knowledge-Sifting." You have to be able to have the wisdom to know the difference between what is good, just, and right.

It doesn't matter which job I observe, whether it is at the doctor's office, the pharmacy, at the military base, or in the grocery store. There is a chasm between decision-makers and the front-line.

The plethora of decisions that an astronaut makes is based on context, just as it is for all of us. We are making decisions based on the fact that change is constant. We need explicit, tacit, and practical wisdom in this day and age.

Robert Sternberg, a contemporary psychometrician, included perspicacity as one of six components of wisdom in his study, "Elements of Wisdom."

The remaining five skills are Reasoning, Sagacity, Learning, Judgement, and the Expeditious use of information.

The perspicacious individual, according to his analysis, is defined as someone who:

- Has intuition.

- Can offer solutions that are on the side of right (ethics) and truth (reality).

- Is able to see through things—read between the lines.

- Has the ability to understand and interpret his or her environment.

https://www.zimbardo.com/a-comprehensive-guide-to-books-by-robert-sternberg/

Wisdom is often recognized as the ability to apply knowledge, experience, and common sense in an insightful manner that leads to sound judgment, effective decision-making, and problem-solving. It's more than just knowing the facts and figures. This involves considering the bigger picture and making thoughtful, empathetic, and forward-thinking choices.

Maturity, self-awareness, and rational thinking in the face of life's challenges are all hallmarks of wisdom. Many cultures link wisdom to spirituality and age.

But there are plenty of elderly people who do not have wisdom either. This, because they did not learn how to transform their wounds into wisdom.

Wisdom is essential for navigating life's complexities and uncertainties. It is wisdom that speaks to you about the consequences of your actions. Just think about how it only takes two years to learn how to speak and the next sixty in how to listen.

Wisdom leads to lifetime fulfillment that contributes to a meaningful and purposeful life through life's difficult moments.

Wisdom is Metanoia, which means "to change one's mind or purpose."

Wisdom is knowing *how* and *why* you think the way you do.

Believe that you are a precious soul with a divine essence. You do not have to be religious or born again or any other label. You just have to believe that there is something inside you that can triumph.

Believe that you are a bright spiritual being gifted with a human experience.

Believe that you can bring about many "Aha" moments.

While the extraordinary power of your perception falsely causes you to believe that you are a hundred percent correct, so it is wisdom and **perspicacity** that can give you extraordinary insight into work and personal life. It is through *perspicacity* that you can arrive at a greater understanding of yourself, others, and have command over your emotions. For this, you cannot live in perpetual chaos. You must be still. It is the inspection of your perceptions that will be the harsh truths that will make you think deeply.

Author's Note

Perception shapes life.

What our brains interpret, judge, sense, feel, and believe becomes part of the schema, identification, and worldview because we deem it to be our indisputable truth.

I have three boxes that I check: □Female. □Southeast Asian. □With a challenge.

My challenge is that my vocal cords do not close, and that makes my voice wiggle and jiggle. Once you know this, then understand that those three checked boxes lend to my schema, identification, biomythography, and my ultimate worldview.

All this to say that everyone has unaware bias. Bias roots itself in the subconscious where schema causes the mind to develop a distinct worldview.

Our worldviews cement from the viewpoint of:

Who I think I am, where I come from, and what values I hold. It encompasses variables, identities, intersections, and self-concepts that either hurt or help change, adaption, and evolution (which, incidentally, was President Marty Apodaca's theme for the NCDA 2025 Global Conference).

I hold a Humanistic worldview, and this means that I believe that everything I encounter enters my life to help me become the best version of myself and for my own good.

My **perspicacity** is for you to code shift in your brain and not view people, places, and things as being bad, wrong, or evil. If you view them as not having knowledge, awareness, or consciousness then you will realize that they have limits. They would do better if they had the knowledge to do better, therefore they are not bad, wrong, or evil.

You can see that a small shift in perspective has the potential to change your whole outlook on how you view, interact, and engage with people, places, and things. One of the most perspicacious things I can say on this page is for you to take a moment to evolve from perception to perspective. This will change your thinking, cause you to find **perspicacity**, and make your life happier.

When I arrive at moments of ***perspicacity***, I am able to reach my full potential. I have learned to train my mind to intentionally move from a negative mindset to a positive mindset, from the Fixed back brain perspective, that is the False Self, to the Frontal Lobe Growth perspective, that is the True Self, so I can experience numerous perspicacious moments.

This is a bottom-up viewpoint, similar to Maslow's theory of needs. I have learned to use fewer words, so I can listen more and because of this, I am viewed as a wise leader. A *guru*.

My Spirit provides me the *voice of wisdom* at work, home, and international stages. Learning how to listen to it is your gateway to making a dramatic shift in consciousness for your wellbeing.

There are many things I share with you so you can lead a happier life. My first book and workbook were written after I graduated from the NCDA Leadership Academy. That book taught people how to self-discover, rectify conflicts, make sensible choices for sustainable impact, and how to work with sensible leadership styles.

It also discussed Interculturalism that I believe to be the wave of the future. My NCDA-funded study yielded significant survey responses regarding Intercultural leadership style as the style that people respect and desire. Since the DEI movement has been eradicated in America, I truly believe that Interculturalism can be the better way to promote new language like Unity, Serenity, and Harmony. An Intercultural leader is a wise leader. Wise thoughts lead to wise actions!

"Activate Success – Tips, Tools, & Insights to Be A Leader In Your Niche" and the accompanying workbook are available on Amazon as paperbacks and Kindle eBooks. This book provides you a myriad of understandings for self-leading and leading others at work and home.

I have not seen a book regarding perception, wisdom, and leadership through the attainment of **Perspicacity.** I wanted to write this second book because the NCDA Board chose me to become Chair of their Leadership Academy, and their trust and confidence enabled me to write about leadership nexus once again.

I was the first to write an article on Common-sense Leadership for the Society for Human Resource Management (SHRM) magazine. I will continue to try and convince their CEO that our disciplines need to be dialoguing and listening to each other.

I invite all leaders to make wisdom and **perspicacity** a priority for decision-making and problem-solving at the table. In the first book I stated that feelings are visitors that come and go, so dwelling on those 'visitors' simply holds us back inside the back brain perspective, and that's not a productive stance. In this book, I am going a step further to encourage you to find yourself beyond the Growth head-brain and into wisdom so you can perform perspicaciously at the table.

Throughout global history, there have been famous gurus from India, China, and Arabia. This brings me to note the difference between **Perspicacity** and *Perspicuity,* where the definition of the former has been discussed at length. The latter, *perspicuity*, refers to clarity in expression or presentation. Both are important and it would benefit people to cultivate both skills.

I am humbled to reach out to you with the hand of my soul.

What if we all saw souls instead of bodies? Wouldn't that be great? I am wise enough to judge people by their character. Their essence. Their soul. Not by the color of anyone's skin. Are you?

Life is short. The way you live your short life is through your perception. You genuinely and authentically do not know what reality is. No one knows. Because everything that happens is perceived and interpreted through a person's unique head (Frontal Lobe, Mid, & Back brains), heart (Cardiac), gut (Enteric), and back brain (Limbic system). Every person experiences life in their own way. Sometimes it works for them and sometimes it does not. When life does not work for them, they know not what to do.

You are influenced by this world by a force that you are not aware of. You automatically become lost in the rat race of this world and unknowingly pursue the mundane. As this occurs repeatedly, an underlying uneasiness in your gut-brain slowly mounts and expresses itself. An innate desire to live a fulfilling and flourishing life aches within you, a yearning that is far beyond the exterior world that has a stronghold on you.

My schema has been distinctly formed as a bicultural immigrant who was born in Southeast Asia and raised in the Western hemisphere. I am able to appreciate and embrace the glimmers of wisdom in both cultures. Without my eastern and western perspectives, I would not be where I am today. People call me a wise leader because I am open to learning, *un*learning, and *re*learning. I am able to set out to make a difference, because I have the wisdom to *know* the difference.

What do you want to be when you grow up?

I remember the first time I was asked what I wanted to be when I grew up. It came from my dad when I was eight years old. Without a pause, I exclaimed, "***I want to be a guru!***"

His head went back as he roared with laughter. I loved his laugh; it was infectious and made everyone smile. My answer dashed out of my mouth so quickly, and I think it's because I would watch the old gurus walking through our town in Maharashtra, India when they made their pilgrimage to the mountains. They were dressed in bright orange fabrics and had white dots painted on their stoic faces that transmitted an aura of wisdom.

They were elder leaders who proselytized that having wisdom was an essential skill for leadership; and leadership was not about being in charge but about looking after those *in our charge*. It's about taking on responsibility.

They looked different from the rest of us, as if they had deviated from the norm. And maybe that was another lesson for me to learn that without deviation from the norm, there is no progress.

While the Indian culture includes a language, folklore, holidays, beliefs, values, norms, behaviors, objects, food, manners, humor, gestures, expectations, biases, self-concept, beauty ideals, approaches to health, the concept of justice, thought patterns, body language, work ethic, personal space, symbols, and spirituality, the Gurus had created a sub-culture that included their own set of wise beliefs and a non-material culture that was rooted in wisdom and **perspicacity**.

Once a year, they passed through my area and stopped to rest at the end of town. They sat beneath the mango trees in a 110-degree heat to cool off a bit, eat, and teach. They were sacred and well revered by the townspeople.

I cannot remember what they taught because it was a long time ago. But I can clearly describe how they made me think. At the young age of eight, those gurus struck something in my brain. I felt sparkles in my brain. I know now that they were, what I now call, "Neuro-sparks." I knew that moment that I wanted to be a guru!

Why aren't there any female gurus?

Why are all the gurus in this world all male?

Whether a professional, student, friend, mother, aunt, or daughter, I believe that some females have incredible insights that need to be shared with this world. It was from a female that I learned that we subconsciously create problems for ourselves but that all miracles begin as problems. Every miracle in books of wisdom started out as problems.

So, what do I want? I want a piece of the pie and I want the recipe too!

This is **perspicacity!**

There are things we remember and other things we simply do not. That's just how our memories work. Or don't work.

How was your SAT experience? An odd question, right? Well, *perspicacity* is the SAT word that I fell in love with during testing. It aptly describes that rare wisdom that enters the frontal lobe perception of the brain. *Perspicacity* brings about those 'aha' moments that can provide great understanding, plus the keenest of acumen.

If you want *perspicacity* in your life, you must be open and willing to receive the wisdom of your inner spirit. Spirit is always on your side; it is a gift, a free friend that will never let you down.

What *perspicacity* does for you, like no other, is to give you great insight into perception. This is *discernment*; it is the wisdom you need to live a life that is closer to the truth and away from an illusionary one (that most people live).

Wisdom is a virtue that you are not born with and it can be obtained through awareness, free will, and lifespan development experiences. Everyone has needs and wants, but few think of introspection and inner work. You are learning lots of things because that's what the brain does. It learns. However, very few take the time to investigate <u>how</u> they are learning and many people fail to use their knowledge for growth, change, and sustainability to become wiser.

The formulation of a human being is based on knowledge, experience, and insight. It will take awareness and intentional practice to arrive at *perspicacity*. Remember, there is no comfort in the growth zone, and there is no growth in the comfort zone. And remember, nothing changes, if nothing changes.

I know personally that many cultures value wisdom and pass on wisdom through storytelling, tales, and fables, just as Aesop did. There are a myriad of perspectives on how to attain wisdom, and the one thing that most cultures agree on is that wisdom brings peace. Stories, tales, and fables all show us good and bad behaviors.

You must look within. Your external world will always be filled with chaos, but you need not absorb that energy; simply observe it instead.

When you suddenly get an ill feeling, look inside your head, heart, and gut brains. Look inside your mind, soul, and spirit. The answers you seek are there. 'And when you accept those answers, your **Spirit Intelligence** increases and raises your energy.'

I believe that there are special neurons in the frontal lobe perception of the brain that give you "sparkling Aha" moments. I call these "*Neuro-sparks*" and they connect just the game that I loved as a child called "Connect the Dots."

Through free will, awareness, intention, and stillness, you can move your thinking from back brain perception to frontal lobe perception and find the Neuro-sparks that can give you *Perspicacity*.

Isn't it time to achieve your full potential and enter a higher realm of what it means to be a human being?

Wisdom is one of those qualities that is difficult to define—because it encompasses intelligence and insight, but oddly enough, people generally recognize it immediately when they encounter it. Wisdom is recognized at work and in personal life; moreover, people unconsciously gravitate towards it.

Experts from many disciplines agree that wisdom is a combination of knowledge, experience, and understanding. It includes accepting life's uncertainties where wisdom and trust emerges. What does it take to call yourself an "expert"? Malcolm Gladwell says you need ten-thousand hours of experience to call yourself an expert. That's a lot of **"knowledge-sifting"**.

Knowledge and experiences are viewed as *cognitive* components of wisdom, while understanding is termed as a *reflective* component. The ability to examine situations, self, benevolence, and empathy are also connected to the wisdom that lends to openness, perspective-taking, intelligence, and *cultural humility* (Cultural humility is a term uses by Melanie Tervalon and Jann Murray-Garcia in 1998 to describe a way of incorporating multiculturalism).

You can gain wisdom from self-reflection and self-evaluation.

Wise people learn from their experiences and past lessons, which affect their present thinking and future perspectives. Wise people are open to new ways of thinking and metacognition, challenging their thinking and using it as a steppingstone to cultivating wisdom and *perspicacity*.

The combination of experiences and education can lead to critical thinking skills and open-mindedness that can help a person navigate through a myriad of contextual situations that hold a number of factors that require wisdom and perspicacity.

A wise person, a guru, considers balance and *im*balance within themselves and others (team, colleagues, family, or friends). They seek to understand, not only their own motives, but the motives of others instead of judging their behavior as good or bad. It is their understanding and respect for diverse perspectives, cultures, and people that provide them with a fulfilling sense of purpose, self-actualization, transcendence, and *perspicacity*.

Psychology Today magazine published 8 elements of wisdom: resilience, kindness, positivity, spirituality, humility, tolerance, creativity, and curiosity. You will find these interspersed in this book.

You don't necessarily have to believe in God or in many gods, as in Hinduism. Religion means group worship and it is not a requirement for wisdom or *perspicacity*. Spirituality is. Believe that there is something grand within.

If you believe in the wise Spirit that resides within you and something greater than yourself that is holy or existential, even though you cannot see that entity, miracles will happen.

An acceptance something greater that resides within you can bring you much closer to peace, comfort, joy, and wellbeing. I am not asking you to believe in something greater than yourself if you do not; I am purely stating that it works for me to know that there is something out there that is free to help me when I ask for help. For some people it is Buddha or Allah, and for others it is Krishna or Jesus, and so on.

Humility, especially cultural humility in this decade, is a universal virtue that must be recognized and emphasized. Cultural humility allows us to accept different cultural perspectives, understanding, and growth through awareness toward an even higher *capacity* of emotional and perspicacious intelligence.

Interculturalism and Cultural Humility help to cut through barriers, racism, ageism, and other-isms that unfortunately exist in every corner of the world. Perhaps through interculturalism and cultural humility we can grow to evolve cultural intelligence, capacity, and change.

There are many roads that you can take in life, but maintaining a relationship with the Spirit of You will help you live your life through faith and wisdom instead of fear and worry. Only you know what you need in life. Only you can choose, through Free Will, what is best for your life. Listen to the spirit, include your spirit when you make your choices, and choose wisely. You have multiple intelligences, so why not increase your Spirit Intelligence too?!

Wisdom is crucial during the time of AI. Do not be distracted by AI, wisdom is more essential than ever before, and it is as rare as a gem. Use wisdom when working with AI. Allow wisdom to guide you in creating AI.

Perspicacity can strengthen this world. You may not know what will happen tomorrow, but if you know who you are today, then the forces of nature will bring you to biological, psychological, social, cultural, technological, and spiritual wisdom.

I firmly believe that ***Perspicacity*** is irrevocably the central component for the advancement of great leaders who have the charge for leadership.

A plethora of authors, male and female, since the beginning of time, have tried to bring us closer to ***perspicacity***. You might not live a fulfilling life without it because you will always feel like something is missing.

Many world cultures profess that gratitude is not only the greatest of virtues but the parent of all others. This is *perspicacity*. It is precisely what you need for those "Aha" moments that transcend you into a higher level of hierarchies (mentioned by Adler, Jung, and Maslow) of being, doing, and having.

It is the preoccupation with the Ego that can cause you to forget your benefits and benefactors, a feeling that this world owes you something for nothing.

Perspicacity can happen when you honestly assess perspectives to try to understand the Self and Others, so you can create a better tomorrow (for yourself and others). I mean, just think of how frightened a blind person may feel if they are reading a braille sign that says, "Do not panic."

Perspicacity is the most powerful of all perceptions because it enhances well-being, strengthens relationships, and shifts irrational focus in the head, heart, and gut brains.

Even William Shakespeare makes a plea: "Lord, please lend me a heart replete with wisdom.".

The Serenity Prayer that asks a higher power to give us the courage to change the things we can and accept the things we cannot, and the *wisdom to know the difference!*

If you never experience *perspicacity* in this lifetime, your subconscious will always feel a void. Regret will make you cling to your past and remind you of the missed opportunities and alternate chances you may have had for a better outcome. Similar to Charles Dicken's story of Ebenezer Scrooge or The Grinch. Do not let it be you.

IF you do not know what to pursue in life right now, please pursue yourself. Wisdom involves cognitive, reflective, and compassionate components. To self-lead and lead others you need practical wisdom (common sense).

The best version of you is the wise and perspicacious self! The moment you learn how to attain **perspicacity** in your own unique brain, great things will most certainly come your way.

Wisdom increases **perspicacity**.

Perspicacity increases intelligence!

Relish the daily change in your brain as you write down thoughts for each day. Be sure to notice the increase in your wise mind and wellbeing.

If you are to activate success for your potential, then you must resist the *downward pull* of the back brain and help the *upward pull* of the frontal lobe in your beautiful brain.

Now is the time to transform into a much better, much wiser, and more perspicacious YOU.

JANUARY

JANUARY 1

Happy New Year! It is the first day of a brand-new year, and for many people it is a day filled with hope.

Celebrate by finding a quiet spot today and bring peace, awareness, and intention into your heart-brain.

There is something deep within you. Accept that your soul and spirit want to help you gain wisdom and *perspicacity* this year. They need a healthy body to live in and the body cannot survive without your help. The fullness and wholeness of your physical awareness are proportional to the depth of commitment you have to your soul and spirit.

Commitment is difficult for many people because they have been conditioned for instant gratification. Studies show that kids who can wait to eat the cookie do much better in life. The *perspicacity* here is good things come to those who can wait.

Discuss 3 things that can give you hope this year.

JANUARY 2

How aware are you?

Cultivate the skill of "Awareness."

Be aware and resist the irrational fantasies
that your back brain perception (also known as the 'monkey' brain)
forces on you in its deceptive ways. Back brain perception distracts you
through feelings and emotions, fear and anxiety, keeps you in a victim
mentality and does not want you to find your purpose.

There will always be someone more intelligent, more beautiful,
and more qualified than you. Does not matter. Keep focused on
understanding your True Self perspective and why you think the way
you do. Question your thinking through calmness and a feeling of
trust in your divine purpose.

Back brain perception: Others need to change; I don't need to change.

Frontal lobe perception: I cannot change others; I can only change
myself.

Perspicacity: Awareness can lead me to **perspicacity**.

How will you cultivate awareness? How can you become more focused
on how you want to respond rather than on feelings and emotions?

JANUARY 3

Something is tugging at you. It tugs at you at the start of each new year. What is it?

The tugging that you feel is what I call **Spirit-Orientation**. It is when the 'Spiritual of You' calls out from the inside through your head, heart, and gut brains.

The Spirit of You desperately wants to help you fulfill your potential and purpose through wisdom and **perspicacity**.

Back brain perception: I need to fit in so I'll continue to spend hours on social media.

Frontal lobe perception: Something is tugging me and that's much more important than social media. I need to spend time to discover what that "tugging" means.

Take time to listen to your *Spirit Orientation* today. What do you hear from the inside?

What **perspicacity** did you find?

JANUARY 4

Your body consists of small parts that make up a whole, and this is the biology of you, while how you think is the psychology of you, beliefs are the culture of you, influences are the social of you, and your values are the spiritual you. I call this your **Individual Schematic Identity**. All those sectors reveal your multiple intelligences.

Theorist Donald Super wrote about the self-concept as *'how you see yourself to be.'* Consciously and subconsciously, you identify with your convictions, expectations, and prejudices. You judge this world harshly and become reactive when the world judges you back that same way. It's always a double standard when it comes to ego.

Back brain perception: I'm not as great as they are.

Frontal lobe perception: I can improve.

Perspicacity: It doesn't serve me well to compare myself to others. I have different interests, skills, and abilities that will be useful for this world.

The Indian culture emphasizes that children can live their lives through parental wishes. Surprisingly, it works well because children are raised to accept that parents know you better than anyone else. They understand that parents want "substance" and not frivolity.

Culture is a massive part of social influences. Norms, customs, language, and behaviors have nuances that differ from nation to nation. Without knowledge, people automatically follow without giving it a single thought.

What influences you? How?

Who has influence over you? Why?

JANUARY 5

Your whole life passes through lifespan stages that are filled with physical and psychological needs.

Theorist Donald Super tells us that each stage of life brings a set of unique questions that the person has to come to grips with. I believe that the Spirit that resides inside you wants to help you navigate through needs, motivations, trust, belongingness, safe environments, efficacy, and purpose.

Perspicacity: When you allow yourself to trust yourself you cultivate a healthy relationship with the Self and who you are at the time, thereby resulting in healthy connections with others.

Who do you trust most in this world? Why?

JANUARY 6

You are living most of your days on automatic pilot. Your subconscious rules, remembers *everything*, and leads your behaviors.

There is a librarian, called the Hippocampus, in your head-brain that keeps track of *everything* that happens to you, and it keeps track of every detail in your subconscious memory. While your conscious mind may not remember everything, you behave a certain way because your subconscious mind is dictating your actions through what I call **Sub-Conscious Puppetry.**

What I mean is that you go about life without conscious awareness. And isn't it so much faster to blurt reactions through your emotions to get immediate gratification?!

Countless theorists emphasize the importance of play and playing.

There are new studies that show that some sociopaths did not have the chance to play during childhood, and this is termed "Play Deprivation." They're not saying that everyone who didn't have the chance to play turns out to be a sociopath. It is a variable that scientists have found in sociopathic personalities. The point here is for children to learn through play and continue learning through play as adults, too.

Perspicacity: You are a child in an adult body; you can develop confidence and character through play. Life is about adaptation and evolution that is based on awareness and intention where the only life you live is the one you create through your perceptions.

What 3 things do you do to play? When have you experienced a shift in consciousness/thinking during playtime? How does Play help you to adapt and evolve into a better version of yourself?

JANUARY 7

As a person enters school, the circle of influence widens and kids begin to compare themselves to others. They take note of what they have the ability to do and what they do not, with regard to skills and aptitude. Kids need your guidance because they don't understand why others can do things and they cannot. Guilt comes into the picture and they need you to increase their self-efficacy.

Perspicacity: You wanted to please the adults around you, but at times, you felt like you disappointed them. In those instances, you wanted unconditional love but may not have gotten it, so the message that cemented in your subconscious Hippocampus was that you would not be loved without pleasing someone.

Who do you want to please? Why?

JANUARY 8

Have you ever been to a middle school bus stop? The cursing is fierce!

They develop self-confidence in their genetic and gifted abilities but feel a sense of inferiority when they cannot do something. They don't fully comprehend yet that everyone has strengths and weaknesses. Groupings begin to formulate based on interests, skills, and abilities. And those that have not found themselves yet get bullied.

This is the age group where children want to get involved in everything from music to dance to sports. They want to try things that their peers are into. Here is where nature and nurture intersect to reveal skills and abilities. Think about it: what if no one gave Yo-Yo Ma a cello?

Perspicacity: You discovered your interests and skills through environmental exposure coupled with genetic ability. For example, if you have the genetic propensity to play the piano, but in your environment, you were never given the chance to play a piano, then that genetic ability would remain undiscovered.

Was there ever a time when you felt inferior? Sometimes this is termed as an "inferiority complex". Where, when, & why? What happened? What did you do? What can be done today for your "inner child"?

JANUARY 9

Do you long to be back in high school?
There is much confusion during the high school years,
because parents want their kids to be something that
they do not want to be. This is the age group where kids are trying to
develop their own sense of *identity* and specific *roles* (son, daughter,
student, friend, cousin) coupled with their place with peers and
society. Peers matter much more than parents.

The teenage brain is not fully developed until the mid-20's. Their
roles and identity-formation helps the teenage brain to navigate their
world. The Sympathetic Nervous System, its Flight and Fight urges,
and hormones are strong. This leaves both parents and teens confused
and flips their communication in disarray.

Back brain perception: It is my house and what I say goes.

Frontal lobe perception: We need to stop yelling and learn how to get
along and live with each other in peace.

Perspicacity: We all have different personalities that have different
needs, so we will need to develop effective communication skills so we
can understand what each of us is saying, wanting, and needing.

What life roles do you enjoy the most? What life roles confuse you and
why? What is your favorite role? Least favorite? Why?

JANUARY 10

Ah, freedom at last! But is freedom a good thing?

Learning how to become independent takes patience. Are you ready to have freedom? Getting along with all types of people is the most challenging skill to cultivate at work and in life. There is much trial and error when it comes to relationships, friendships, and intimacy. Some young people are not ready for adulting and stay home until their 30's.

Back brain perception: Now I can do anything I want.

Frontal lobe perception: It feels good to have a job and have some financial freedom from my folks.

Perspicacity: I have to learn the difference between needs and wants. I realize that my parents want the best for me, so I will work with them instead of against them. And I also understand the part that hormones play in my feelings and emotions.

How do you cultivate healthy relationships? Do you have a healthy relationship with yourself? Because if you do not like yourself, then you will not like anyone else.

Be aware of patterns in situations where your hormones take over your logical thinking. Do not let your hormones make decisions for you!

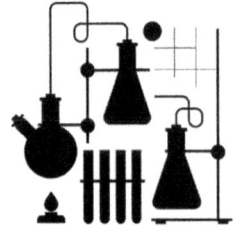

JANUARY 11

You may have learned in your high school physics class that change is constant. This is true externally and internally. ~74 thousand thoughts rotate through your head-brain each day. Only you know how you decide which thoughts to pay attention to and which ones to ignore. It is your *perception* that is responsible for your how you think, feel, and react. Your perceptions are the basis of your worldview, decision-making, and problem-solving.

Back brain perception: Why can't people just agree with everything I say?

Frontal lobe perception: I learned in physics class that Change is Constant, which means that Nothing is Permanent, so after my anger subsides, I can calm down to think rationally rather than emotionally.

Perspicacity: The change may be better than I imagined. I need to cultivate an open mind and not feel so negative about change. I can transform my negative energy and consider other perspectives while I look for wisdom in my circumstances.

Try to explain your feelings/emotions instead of expressing them through anger. You will find solutions instead of arguments.

What is the most liberating thought that you've ever had? How did it make you wiser? What are the great benefits of **perspicacity** for you, and how will it positively affect your work and life?

JANUARY 12

You remember your parents' first names, and you remember your grandparents' first names, but do you remember your *great*-grandparents' first names? Most people do not.

The people that you work with and family that are between the ages of 70 and 100 are losing their physical attributes. They are forced to retire or are neglected by certain cultures.

I do not understand Ageism at all, because <u>everyone</u> is going to get old. This stage arrives quickly. Take advantage of the wisdom from your elders. Ask them questions and seek their answers. Pass on their stories. It is history.

Back brain perception: I do not have time for old people.

Frontal lobe perception: I am thankful for my family, young and old.

Perspicacity: I need to be available to dialogue with elders and listen to their storytelling. I am sure I can learn much from them. After all, I am carrying their genes.

What stories have you heard from your parents? Grandparents? Great-grandparents? How have those stories affected you? What wisdom did you find in their storytelling?

JANUARY 13

Be aware (or beware too) of the life stage you are in!

⑦

Which stage are you in right now?

Each person, regardless of who they are or the culture they were born in has the exact same human needs. We all have the exact physiological and psychological needs.

Our mindset emerges through our stories. Storytelling emerges through our unmet needs. We all have the disposition to tell life's stories and unfortunately they most always speak through Ego's point of view. It is through our own eyes, ears, nose, mouth, head, heart, and gut that we believe our stories to be undoubtedly the truth a 100% of the time.

Whether you are at your highest point of victory or your lowest point of defeat, the stories you tell yourself will either activate or deactivate your potential in moving forward towards wisdom and *perspicacity*.

Do you feel like you are stuck? BTW, "stuck" is a proper clinical term. How can you become unstuck? Be aware of the story you tell yourself every day. The repetition of that story will keep you stuck in a certain way of thinking and believing.

Why am I not getting what I want? Why do other people get things before me? Change your story. Change your mindset. Change your life.

JANUARY 14

You were born as a blank slate with a set of genes from your parents.

Ater you were born, your parents conditioned you to follow norms and customs. You wake up, go to work, eat, sleep, and repeat. Those behaviors became habits and patterns that cemented themselves into your muscle memory.

This means that you go through most of your waking hours automatically like an AI robot that has been programmed.

For 22 years, you gained the knowledge you needed to survive independently in this world. Automatic behavior ensued. Then, a day arrived where you felt unfulfilled?

How come you noticed this uncomfortable feeling that moment?

It is because you neglect the spirit that lives within you. Your ego distracts you towards meeting your needs through comparing, contrasting, jealousy, and vengeance. Once you've done all of those, you are left feeling empty.

What I am trying to say to you is that you have operationally defined each category in your life through intellectualism or emotional validity, however, they are simply not enough for you to feel complete.

What can you do to listen to your inside voice, soul, and spirit? Fill in the missing piece and peace.

JANUARY 15

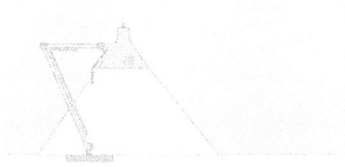

"We lift ourselves by our thoughts.
If you want to enlarge your life, you must first enlarge your thoughts
about it and of yourself. Hold the ideal of yourself everywhere you go."

~Orison Swett Marden, 1850-1924
author and founder of Success magazine.

What does this quote mean to you?

JANUARY 16

Perspicacity gives you wisdom, insight, and confidence that I call "**Inner Command**." This *inner command* will help you to get much closer to your soul, spirit, and feeling fulfilled.

One day, you will wake up feeling automatic joy. Why am I feeling this way? That is a good thing!

No one can <u>make</u> you happy. Joy emerges from an understanding of your soul. When that day comes, you will feel a deep connection with your Spirit. Your *perspicacity* will have replaced fear and anxiety. This **Spirit Orientation** will help you to overcome blocks and barriers, and even all the -isms that are out there.

If you could create a "how to" manual for human beings, what 5 things would you include in it? Why? How would it help human beings?

JANUARY 17

Uncertainty duplicates.

The truth is that no one is certain about anything. Most people are just making it up as they go and move about their days. Accept the reality that nothing in the future is guaranteed, no matter how many goals or mentors we collect.

Perspicacity: You make decisions and problem-solve automatically based on your emotions. Question emotions to illicit what they are trying to tell you, then bring yourself from the back to the front of the brain to inspect and introspect.

You do not have to be a religious or spiritual person to listen to your inside voice. Are you willing to trust the Spirit within you instead of entertaining your emotions? You must! Your spirit will instruct you to take the right path without wallowing in your feelings and emotions.

What do you feel is the most effective way to make a positive mark on this world?

JANUARY 18

What is reality?

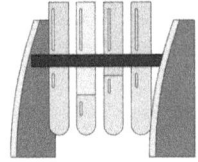

No one knows what reality is because everyone is sensing, perceiving, judging, and interpreting what they perceive through their senses and brains. Did you know that what you smell goes directly into the Hippocampus? Smell is tied to your memory storage!

Back brain perception: I am a victim of my circumstances.

Frontal lobe perception: I can control certain things, while others are impossible to control.

Perspicacity: I have a certain worldview that I hold on to tightly. It has been created through my upbringing, values, beliefs, assumptions, and biases. Through awareness and intention, I can understand diverse perspectives.

What 3 things can you do to get as close to reality as possible?

JANUARY 19

What comes to mind when you hear the word "Culture"?

You are thinking of someone born in another country or that looks different or that has an accent, but did you know that every family has a culture of their own? Yes! Each family has a certain way of doing things through beliefs, values, preferences, and traditions. Organizations also have a certain way of doing things through their mission, vision, and values, just like families do.

So, culture has very much to do with people and their beliefs and values!

Perspicacity: Culture is a mindset. Culture consists of norms and values that cause groups to behave in a certain way when they are together and apart. The family you come from contributes to your reality.

What is your family's culture? Name 2 traditions, 2 values, and 2 beliefs.

How does your home culture affect your workplace culture?

Through beliefs, values, and traditions, you could create any reality you wish.

JANUARY 20

Nature or Nurture? Genetics or Environment?

Internal and external factors help you evolve as a human being. Your environmental factors can either be risky or can be protective factors that affect your internal safety, resiliency, and self-esteem. Some people are lucky to have a safe childhood environment, while others have extremely traumatic childhoods.

Do not misconstrue high expectations with positive thinking. Positive thinking comes from optimism (personality and temperament), while high expectations come from beliefs and schema. The quality of your beliefs will serve to increase the optimism (and dopamine) inside your personality and, thereby, your capacity.

During your younger lifespan stages, you had an external locus of identity. You saw yourself as others saw you. The beliefs and expectations you had in the past had an impact on your thoughts and behaviors. You cannot pretend ONLY to have high expectations because you must believe in your ability to achieve those expectations.

Perspicacity: Optimism yields achievement and not the other way around. It is not about your feelings but what you think you are capable of.

What is your self-talk? Are messages coming from the irrational monkey brain or the rational frontal lobe perception?

Are you optimistic or pessimistic? Are you open or closed-minded? Are you nervous or confident? Are you conscientious or undutiful?

JANUARY 21

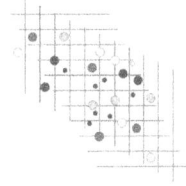

I believe that Maslow's bottom-up theory states that each level is a catalyst that helps a person move up to the next level. For example, the importance of satisfying physiological needs is the catalyst to meeting four psychological needs. Belonging is the *catalyst* for activating self-esteem.

Many studies since then have indicated the importance of belonging, thereby causing organizations to focus on multicultural — a movement that comes out of the Civil Rights Movement in America that supports Black people.

However, political leaders have discarded multiculturism, leaving people feeling angry and panicked. Out of anger and panic, some people have chosen violence and retaliation (back brain perception behaviors). This completely goes against Gandhi and MLK's philosophy of Passive Resistance Nonviolence.

Perspicacity: Most behaviors are fear-based, therefore the emotional brain needs to be guided and controlled otherwise it can create havoc. The removal of diversity programs will make space for something better. Believe. Something greater is coming. If you have faith, then continue believing.

How can you create a better understanding of differing perspectives?

How can you create a sense of belongingness at work without using the words "Black, White, Brown, Yellow, or Red"?

JANUARY 22

Life is all about relationships. If you want to live on Earth, then you must learn how to live and work with all kinds of people. The focus you have on yourself makes your back brain perception feel great, but it's extremely unproductive.

If you have many conflicts with others, then it's time to introspect and learn to understand yourself. If you don't understand yourself, how can you understand others? You can't! When you don't understand yourself, you end up misconstruing 'offense' as 'disrespect'. Just because you feel offended does not make you right! You will end up accusing another for the truth they perceive. You won't understand that your truth is *YOUR* truth, and their truth is *their* truth. Remember, life is all about perception. And wisdom is all about turning that perception into something intelligent.

Perspicacity: Work hard to understand others without getting offended. Offense is not disrespect; it's just perception.

Are you listening to understand others without bias or cognitive distortions? How?

JANUARY 23

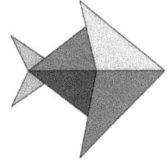

You have a great toolbox in your genes. Find out what your interests, skills, and abilities are and find out what you are passionate about. Stop being jealous of people that have different skills and abilities compared to you. Stop comparing and judging.

Back brain perception: I wish I was just like her. I will make my hair like hers and dress like her, so I can become her.

Frontal lobe perception: It's wonderful that she has certain gifts. I am happy for her and will give her compliment next time I see her.

Perspicacity: We are all different. We all have a purpose. I just need to find mine so I don't covet.

How can you value multiplicity of interests, skills, and abilities in the workplace, home, and community?

JANUARY 24

Interview yourself today.

Capability comes from competency. What can you do to make yourself more competent?

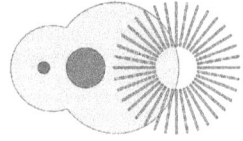

....
....

Is caring about social change a competency? Why or why not?

....
....

What can your colleagues and family members do to make you feel valued?

....
....

What can the system do to make you feel included? How does this relate to justice?

....
....

JANUARY 25

You worry about what you want to be at the end of the year, but you forget that you are somebody *today*!

Pretend you are an inventor. What would you invent that could make your life easier? Write to me and let me know what you came up with!

JANUARY 26

The juncture of AI and law will soon intersect. AI-powered justice is transforming the legal landscape. To ensure this revolution has the highest ethical standards and delivers impartial outcomes, new jobs will be emerging. AI legal oversight officers will be the new CEOs who will be held responsible for how AI is used in the complexities of the judicial system.

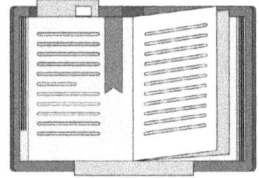

You will soon see job descriptions for AI Legal Quality Assurance Officer, AI Risk Officer, AI Compliance Officer, AI Transparency Officer, AI Ethics Officer, AI Integration Specialist, AI Strategy Consultant, AI Training and Development Specialist, AI Financial Officer, AI Innovation Specialist, and AI Policy Advisor.

How will you prepare for this AI revolution? Think about this quote as your answer. "Be open to revise any system, scrap any method, abandon any theory if the success of the job requires it."

If you could switch jobs with anyone for a month, what job would that be?

JANUARY 27

Fighting is not the first lesson of martial arts.

The first lesson of martial arts is to learning *how to fall*.

When you become unfearful of falling, then you can commit to anything that comes your way!

Lifespan developmental stages depend on achievements, interventions, and preventions. Beliefs, behaviors, knowledge, and skills are all achievement outcomes, but which of these can also prevent things from happening?

Perspicacity: Focus on *who* and *what* you are becoming through what you *prevent*. There are things you achieve because of what you *prevent*.

What things do you prevent? What things need intervention?

If you had to fight for one cause for the rest of your life, what would it be and why?

JANUARY 28

Knowledge, skills, beliefs, and behaviors are tied to wisdom.

Focus on your mindset as preparation for long-term triumphs.

The achievement of short-term goals will get you to your long-term dream.

Perspicacity: Focusing on mindset that has the potential to bring about wisdom.

What keeps you engaged in short-term goals?

What keeps you engaged in long-term goals?

What is one behavior, belief, and habit that you need to change to achieve goals and *perspicacity*?

JANUARY 29

Harvard Law School – Program on Negotiation taught me six guidelines for getting a "Yes" during mediation, negotiation, and conflict resolution.

They are:

1. Separate your view of the person from the issue.
2. Focus on interests, not on positions.
3. Learn to manage emotions at the table.
4. Express appreciation for and encourage diverse perspectives.
5. Put a positive spin on your message.
6. Escape the action and reaction cycle that instantly shows up from the back-brain.

Seven percent are the words, thirty-eight percent are the tone and pace, and fifty-five percent are body language.

Your goal in any relationship is ZOPA. The Zone of Probable Agreement.

Understand multiple viewpoints. Adapt your emotions to situational awareness. Understand everybody's motivations.

Appeal to six basic human needs:

1. Certainty
2. Uncertainty
3. Significance
4. Love

5. Growth

6. Giving

The brain loves novelty, so sometimes it misconstrues conflict as novelty and excitement. How do you resolve conflicts? What have you learned from resolving conflicts at work and in your personal life? How can you prevent conflicts?

JANUARY 30

A common mistake that systems make is that they provide opportunities without offering corresponding support.

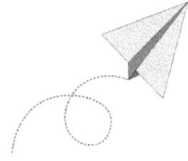

Opportunity and Support go hand in hand, but some rarely see it this way. Without support, you might fail in the opportunity that is offered to you. The ***perspicacity*** here is that it's not necessarily your fault that you feel out of balance.

Many professional associations offer many opportunities but fail to provide support, training, or onboarding. They assume that people know about the chain of command, rules of order, how to interpret an Excel sheet, how to write an agenda, how to write the Minutes of a meeting, or even emotional intelligence.

Perspicacity: The same goes for providing too much support without opportunities for people to shine.

How can you create an opportunity for yourself if nothing presents itself?

What kind of support(s) do you need at work? At home?

JANUARY 31

The absence of an issue does not imply contentment and well-being.

Systems need to understand the importance of lifespan development because their employees have different *needs based on different stages.* Leaders know about generational differences, but I've never heard leaders talk about the needs of the stages -- initiative, autonomy, generativity, and stagnation from the Lifespan Development Stage theory.

Perspicacity: Focus on understanding what each stage *needs* regarding lifespan development stages, not just through blanket generic generations.

What Lifespan Development Stage are you in? What's the difference between needs and wants? What do you *need* to get through this stage?

What do you *need* to do to increase your wisdom, **perspicacity**, and intelligence?

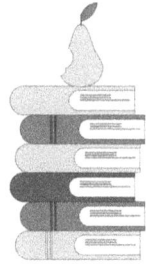

FEBRUARY

FEBRUARY 1

Are you a control freak?

The urge to control (everything and everyone) comes from the back 'monkey' brain that experiences fear and anxiety.

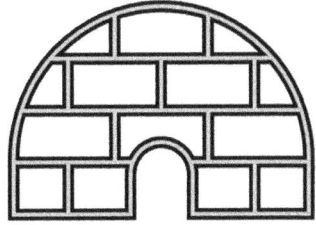

How is your Locus of Control? Is it out of control, or are you in control of what you want to control?

What are 3 things that you can control at work?

What are 3 things that you can control in life?

What are 3 things that you *cannot* control? How can you cope healthfully with those things that you cannot control? It takes a certain amount of wisdom to know the difference between what you can change and what you cannot. Do you have the wisdom to know the difference?

FEBRUARY 2

All that you perceive is initiated from your memories, and I must tell you that, as a species, we have terrible memories. If everything we think and do stems from memory, then are we living in a mirage?

You, me, and everyone else are living a life that is not reality. We are making decisions and solving problems out of what we can remember, not from what actually happened. It's our version where we totally believe our story from our memory, schema, bias, and point of view.

What is one story that you remember but another person remembers differently? How did it make you feel?

Is there a story that you tell that is different from the one your siblings or parents tell? How does it make you feel?

Perspicacity: Each person is telling their truth. It may not necessarily be *your* truth. It's *their* truth. It's not constructive to get mad or offended at people who are revealing a narrative from their lens. This piece should help you a great deal in reducing your blood pressure and being open to listening to and accepting that what they are stating or writing is their individual and unique truth.

Gustave Flaubert once said, "There is no truth. There is only perception."

Every person that brings their perspective to the table thinks they are 100% correct! Their story is what they believe to be the absolute truth. How can you listen to understand without getting offended?

FEBRUARY 3

The monkey back brain perception gets in the way of your happiness. How? It is emotional, irrational, and reactive.

If you are not aware of your unreasonable back monkey brain, you will spend your whole life making decisions based on emotions and impulses. If you have many conflicts and misunderstandings in your life, then that's where you are. If you are offended at everything, then that's where you are.

Perspicacity: I must make a change in myself, if I want to see a change. This is wisdom. I have the perspicacity to know the difference.

It takes time for thoughts to move from the back brain perception to the frontal lobe perception. Time is your friend, especially during emotionally heightened situations.

Train yourself to be calm and quiet during emotional moments so you can allow heated thoughts to go from the back to the front of your brain. Time will also give you the peace you need so you can listen to your spirit. A time out for adults is just as beneficial as when you give it to your kids.

What can you do to recognize your back-brain's chaotic thinking?

Consider your emotional responses. Name 3 things that bring you contentment. How?

FEBRUARY 4

Your body has a "to do" list every day.

If you have a paper cut, it goes on the body's list and gets healed in a few days. If you have a bruise, then that body makes note of it and heals in a couple of days. Healing does not happen in seconds. Healing takes time. Papercuts and bruises don't heal overnight but take time.

You don't spend your hours staring at your paper cuts and bruises. You trust that they will heal, and they miraculously do heal!

You believe in that which can be unseen.

The mind-body connection is real. What you think, you become. What you believe transpires.

If you believe that your body can heal, then can you believe that your mind can heal? How can you help your mind to heal?

FEBRUARY 5

This month is the month for hearts, flowers, and love.

What are 2 things that you love about your job?

What are 2 things that you love about your life?

FEBRUARY 6

Trust. Loyalty. Respect.

If you mess one up, it will affect the others.

How do you build trust?

How do you show that you are a loyal employee?

How do you show that you are a loyal friend?

How do you show this world that you respect yourself?

What values cause you to respect others?

FEBRUARY 7

An overactive imagination creates your greatest fears. Refrain from giving in to false evidence that appears real. Fears come from the back and emotional brain. In your younger stages, you didn't have the life skills and life values to understand.

Life skills include things like integrity, self-awareness, a positive attitude, a strong work ethic, good interpersonal skills, good organizational skills, excellent written and verbal skills, listening skills, ambitions, emotional intelligence, and, did I say, a strong work ethic. (Ha!).

Your work ethic is not a reaction to external expectations; it is an internal commitment to producing work that resonates with the standard of excellence that you have set for your mind, soul, and spirit.

Life Values: honest, confident, dependable, self-motivated, flexible, accountable, resourceful, action-oriented, presentable, culturally fit, passionate, goal-oriented, diplomatic, humble, independent, intelligent, disciplined, proactive, empathetic, and did I say culturally fit?

Life skills and values are <u>transferable</u> skills that can transfer from job to job, relationship to relationship, and context to context.

What 3 life skills do you have? Where do you use them the most?

What are your 3 life values that you will never compromise?

FEBRUARY 8

In life, you have to be patient. Patience is a virtue.

The Spirit of You wants this year to be your renovation year. It may be messy or confusing, but that's because it's in the creation and forming stage. You are art in progress.

Be kind and patient with yourself, even when it is hard.

Your effort matters where mistakes are lessons; there are no failures where failures are part of success. Give yourself grace and permission to make mistakes, but don't forget that you also have the obligation to learn from them and not repeat them.

Stay true to who you are, no matter what the circumstances.

Help someone whenever you can.

Patience is a virtue that can be practiced while waiting in line or waiting for your food.

Perspicacity: I am conditioned to want things instantaneously! It's because I live in an immediate gratification society, but not everything works on an instant timeline. I did wait for four years to earn a degree. I devoted time to learning how to ride a bike, swim, and play an instrument. Good things take time. I am able to train myself to be patient. What are 3 things that you had to wait for? Was it worth the wait?

FEBRUARY 9

Each snowflake is configurated differently. We are as different as snowflakes. Train yourself for solidarity and not for charity, so that you can work together with others in a partnership for the good of everyone.

Through patience and *perspicacity*, you can have closure with unfinished endings, messy relationship conclusions, and words unsaid. It was Kahlil Gibran that said, "our worst fault is our preoccupation with the faults of others".

How are you disciplining yourself in your pursuit of *perspicacity*?

FEBRUARY 10

It's time to ditch manipulation. It's a survival mechanism that helps you meet your needs, but it makes more work for you because people get hurt and then you have to go backwards to mend situations.

Perspicacity: Anytime you feel like manipulating people, places, or things, ask yourself this question: What is resonating inside of me to cause such feelings to occur? Are they accurate? Am I inflating (or deflating) something? Why is my ego feeling defensive?

The *perspicacity* is always to introspect because the answers are within!

The Spirit Self does not need to manipulate others.

Introspect and figure out why you have the need to manipulate people, places, and things. The introspection of individual perceptions comes from Adlerian therapy practices.

FEBRUARY 11

The workplace is often referred to as "the concrete jungle." It breathes and breeds fierce competition through carnivorous hierarchies. It is demandingly discontent.

This environment can either make you want to do less or turn you into an animal inside that concrete jungle. If this jungle causes you stress and burnout, then you can move. You are not a stationary tree.

A few TED Talks to watch:

1. How to gain control of your time by Laura Vanderkam
2. The first 20 hours–how to learn anything by Josh Kaufman
3. Inside the mind of a master procrastinator by Tim Urban
4. Grit–the power of passion and perseverance by Angela Lee Duckworth
5. The brain-changing benefits of Exercise by Wendy Suzuki

Name 2 TED Talks that you watch to motivate yourself.

Name 2 Podcasts that you listen to motivate yourself.

FEBRUARY 12

If happiness is your priority, remember that no one else can give you lasting happiness. True happiness comes from within and from the Spirit of You.

Social media gives great examples of *lust*. Know the difference between lust and love.

Lusting will have you crying over a closed door that has nothing behind it. Remember, you are not a product of your circumstances; you are a product of your hormones and perceptions.

"But, Dr. Sujata, she's the perfect woman for me, even though she's married and has kids." Use common sense and connect the dots. Our feelings and thoughts feel real, but that doesn't mean they are *true*.

Give an example of lust and one of love. How did those make you feel? What were the outcomes of both instances?

FEBRUARY 13

Confidence comes from empathy. You can be both confident and kind instead of confident and arrogant. How kind or caring are you to people who cannot do anything for you?

Seek to understand *first*, then to be understood (as Stephen Covey says). Work and life are about mastering self-discipline and self-control; when you look inward, it will deter you from blaming others all the time.

Perspicacity: Gang up on the issue collaboratively and without blame or cynicism.

How do you stay focused on the issue and not on the personality?

How do you develop a solution-oriented mindset?

FEBRUARY 14

Have you heard the IALAC story? IALAC stands for "I am loveable and capable." It is a story written by Sidney Simon. It's a concept that refers to self-esteem and how someone feels about themselves.

The size of a person's IALAC can indicate how good they feel about themselves and can be affected by how others interact with them. The IALAC story can be used as a guiding principle for personal growth and healing. It can help people develop a positive self-image, build healthy relationships, and foster self-compassion.

Google the story and discuss the impact that this story has on you.

What two things do you love about yourself?

How is your self-esteem? What 3 things can you do to increase your self-esteem?

How can you measure your self-compassion?

FEBRUARY 15

The two most important days are: *"The day that you were born and the day that you figure out why,"* said Mark Twain.

When you realize that the whole world reflects how you think and based on your worldview, then you will soon realize that no one is against you.

What things can you do today to figure out why you were born?

FEBRUARY 16

The degree to which you can grow and evolve is directly proportional to the amount of truth you can accept about yourself. (Please read that sentence thrice).

There are things you know about yourself, and there are things that others know about you that you cannot see. Inquire only if you are prepared to hear their response. Don't ask them if you're going to berate them and say you feel disrespected. That's childish, and it means you're not open to accepting their truth about you, causing you to get angry, storm out, and call family meetings for talks where you alone are doing the talking while they roll their eyes. Yes?

Be open and willing to hear the truth from others without getting defensive. Are you there yet?

You suffer because you have a blind spot, and you are unwilling to listen to the wisdom and *perspicacity* that others can offer you.

Are you trying to avoid the truth about yourself? Why?

FEBRUARY 17

There are many 'effects' in psychology. The Dunning-Kruger Effect is a type of cognitive bias where people with little expertise or ability assume they have superior expertise or ability.

This overestimation stems from insufficient self-awareness regarding their knowledge limitations.

How can you work with such a boss or co-worker? Allowing people to 'save face' is a construct in a myriad of world cultures. How can you bring about your truth without pointing a person out through public humiliation or 'calling out'? Can you 'call in' instead?

DH Lawence once said, "Do not be a slave to your own idea of yourself."

FEBRUARY 18

Studies on Emotional Intelligence (EI) state that you need five things to be successful:

Self-awareness, self-regulation, motivation, empathy, and social skills.

To do the above, you need the capacity to identify, manage, evaluate, and understand your emotions. Just because you feel a certain emotion doesn't make you correct! Great leaders have cultivated the skill of Self-leading, so they introspect first. They ask themselves: "What is resonating inside of me that is causing these emotions to erupt here and now; how can I manage them as a conscious leader?"

How do you self-regulate your emotions? How do you self-soothe?

How do you self-lead before leading others?

You need to boost a client's self-awareness and motivation.

What feedback approach do you choose, and why?

FEBRUARY 19

If two people agree on everything, one of them is unnecessary!

Goodness, if you want your partner to agree on everything, then marry yourself! Everyone has a different brain; therefore, everyone thinks and focuses on distinct aspects of what you have said. In short, everyone has a different perception. Do not berate them for having a brain different from yours. Instead, through calmness and understanding, ask them to explain their thinking so you can gain more clarity. Get this!

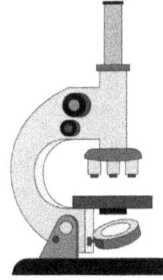

Look into the microscope of your heart and think of a situation from the past where you passed judgment on another person's perception. What happened? How would you do things differently?

FEBRUARY 20

Ethos (spirit, philosophy, principles), Pathos (feelings, values, emotions), and Logos (reasons, evidence, research).

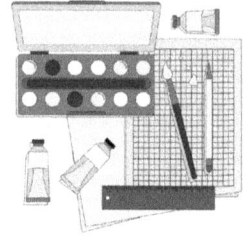

Ethos is the consideration of character, credibility, and ethics to inform or persuade.
Character is what you are made of and what shows up during the second or third try.

Pathos refers to emotions and passion to inform or persuade.

Logos is about logical reasoning and evidence to inform or persuade.

In work and life, you will spend most of your time either informing or persuading. Using all three approaches will help you to convey your message much better.

One-third of your colleagues/family/friends/audience will want to hear Ethos, a third will want to hear Pathos, and a third will want to hear Logos.

Use all three to your advantage when you are trying to inform or persuade.

Make sure you know all the relevant theories and master relevant techniques. Be sure to touch a human soul by showing them that you are also a human soul.

Be cautious not to show privilege. Privilege is when you think something is not an issue because it's not a problem for you.

Show empathy. When you show empathy for someone's experience, please make sure that you believe them in the way *they* see things and not how you imagine it to be. Restate what they say to ensure clarity.

How can you include Ethos, Logos, & Pathos in your presentations? Professionally and personally.

FEBRUARY 21

Whether at work or in your personal life, eventually, you will face an ethical dilemma.

The back brain perception will have you do what is easy, not what is right.

Listen to what you are justifying in your narrative/inside voice. Most of the time, people justify their conduct through Defense Mechanisms such as denial, projection, displacement, reaction formation, sublimation, regression, repression, etc.

1. Identify who the hero is in the story you are telling yourself.
2. Who is the villain?
3. Determine the ethical or moral issue.
4. Determine why and how this needs to be solved.

Healthy relationships require honesty. Before pointing any fingers, learn to self-lead and self-inspect your thinking.

Name a time when you found yourself in an ethical dilemma.

What happened? What did you do? What was the outcome? What will you do differently next time?

FEBRUARY 22

What qualities can you develop that can make collaborating better?

....
....

What qualities can you develop that can make cooperating better?

....
....

Are you reliable and trustworthy? How and where?

....
....

Do you act on your initiative, or do you stuff tasks in the bottom drawer? Why or why not?

....
....

Do you work well under pressure, or do you complain?

The ***perspicacity*** here is: when you voice a complaint, always state a solution!

....
....

Are you adaptable to change? Why or why not?

....

....

Are you getting micro-credentials and learning new skills?

....

....

Do you ask questions for clarity instead of assuming? How and where?

....

....

More wisdom: Put this all together, and you will be Intercultural.

Being intercultural will put you miles ahead of others. If you have these qualities, then be sure to rewrite your job description and resume.

FEBRUARY 23

There are six P's that make your brand unforgettable.

1. People
2. Pain
3. Promise
4. Process
5. Price
6. Perspicacity

Are you identifying your target market?

....
....

Do you understand their struggle?

....
....

Are you creating their solution?

....
....

Are you with them each step of the way?

....
....

Is your price based on the value you bring to the table?

....

....

Are you using wisdom, insight, discernment, and common sense?

....

....

FEBRUARY 24

Impression management is an important construct at work and in one's personal life.

How is my appearance?

Why do I choose these outfits to wear?

What do I enjoy wearing, and how do those clothes make me feel?

Why do these clothes and accessories affect my emotional state of being?

How will I define success this year? Success means different things to different people. Listen to your Spirit when you define what success means to you.

How will I manage stress differently this year? Stress emerges out of fear and anxiety, so be sure to call on the Spirit to help you to see clearly.

How will I self-care? Not too much. Not too little. Moderation is key.

How will I maintain work and life in balance? Remember, everyone has Needs, so be transparent, communicate, and love.

FEBRUARY 25

Use this page as a vision board to draw your thoughts and how you have evolved your perspicacity.

FEBRUARY 26

Prioritize effective communication; it minimizes workplace and life conflicts.

Do not consider yourself to be an adult unless you know how to effectively communicate, apologize genuinely, speak your truth, and accept accountability without blaming someone else for your choices.

Today, I want you to think about and write down 3 things that can bring peace into your workplace and 3 things that can bring peace into your personal life.

FEBRUARY 27

What are 3 things that you wish people understood about you, and why did you choose those things?

FEBRUARY 28

Increase your productivity!

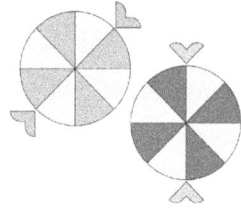

1. Look at the weather and pick out your clothes the night before.
2. Make a list of daily tasks that must be accomplished that day.
3. If a nap increases your output per unit of time, then it is productive to take a nap.
4. Burnout happens when you do not rest. Try not to quit. Rest instead. The urge to quit is simply your brain in flight mode.
5. Compare yourself to who you were yesterday and not to anyone else. It does not make sense to compare your chapter five to someone else's chapter ten.
6. Be an adult and accept constructive feedback graciously. You do not have to get defensive because it's just their opinion.
7. If you want to change something, then measure it. If you cannot measure something, then let it go.
8. If you want to break a habit, then track it.
9. If you fail to plan, then you plan to fail.

How else can you increase your productivity? Performance? Perspicacious intelligence?

MARCH

MARCH 1

Gusty March winds are here. Don't get blown away.
Stay grounded.

Questions to ask during a job interview.

1. I have the job description in front of me. Which of these
    responsibilities is your immediate priority?
2. How would you rank these responsibilities?
3. How would you define doing an excellent job in this
    position?
4. What type of person thrives in your company?
5. Are there any responsibilities or areas that I need to clarify to
    confirm my suitability for this particular job?
6. What does your company value?

Do not overuse professional jargon or acronyms. For example,
BTW, IDK about…. Be transparent and down-to-earth because your
authenticity is what you will be bringing to work every day.

Each of us is defined by a collection of behaviors that enter through a
doorway. Our conduct speaks louder than the words we utter.

Make sure you know yourself well so you can articulate your interests,
strengths, weaknesses, and values. When you do this, you are alleviating
your fears and the fears of those hiring you.

There's no denying that the pandemic changed the world profoundly.
AI advances technology rapidly, and corporations are pushing to

optimize performance without addressing a host of new workplace anxieties due to a lack of time.

Fear is an aggressive predator in the workplace. Most behaviors are fear-based. Leaders do not always know how to offer a sharp vision for a fear-free company culture. This is one area where you can be instrumental in creating a high-trust, high-performance culture for your company!

What is one thing you can do to improve your pitch?

MARCH 2

Psychological hacks.

Argue intelligently, not defensively. If you are in an argument, stay quiet, and when they are done speaking, stay silent and just stare at them.

If you want to de-escalate someone's anger, ask them questions about numbers or something personal.

If you want someone to get nervous, look at their forehead.

If you want someone to tell you the truth, make them laugh before you ask the question.

When you are in a group, and someone makes fun of you, ask them if they are okay.

If someone interrupts you while you are speaking, continue to speak over them.

At work and in life, praise people behind their backs.

Instead of asking, "Do you have any questions?" asking people, "What questions do you have?" works much better.

Greet everyone you know with a genuine smile.

Which one do you like the best? Why?

Try one out today.

MARCH 3

Career mistakes.

1. Forgetting to network. You don't have to be an extroverted social butterfly, but you can make connections with like-minded people.
2. Not being prepared. Really?
3. Assuming you know everything. Because you think you have arrived at the top of the mountain, there is no other place to go but down.
4. Not listening to others because you think you know it already. Because everyone knows something you do not.
5. Throwing away business cards. Never.
6. Being late. Why? Set your alarm. When you are on time, you are late.
7. Finding office gossip exhilarating. It can become an addiction.
8. Oversharing. Because no one at work really cares.
9. Dressing unprofessionally. HR will tell you to never wear capris to work.
10. Not proofreading your emails. Read those to the very end.
11. Not learning from mistakes.
12. Not having a mentor. Does not matter how old you are.
13. Not being a coach.
14. Having a negative attitude. Because you can never move positively with a negative anything.

15. Not asking for help. Don't allow pride to get in the way of progress.
16. Bonus: Forgetting to send thank-you notes.

Where do you need to improve?

MARCH 4

The battle you must be aware of each day is the one with Ego versus your Spirit.

Ego craves to serve itself. Ego thrives on outer recognition.

Ego views life as a competition. Ego always wants to preserve itself.

Ego only sees outwards. Ego feels lack. Ego hates disappointment.

Ego lusts. Ego enjoys causing pain.

Your spirit seeks to include others. Your spirit craves inner authenticity.

Your spirit views life as a gift. Your spirit looks to preserve others.

Your spirit knows about abundance. Your spirit is drawn to empathy, love, healing, and wisdom.

Your spirit is reticent. Your spirit wants you to have perspicacity.

******

How aware are you of your Ego self?

How aware of you of the Spirit of You?

What can you do to bring more awareness into your brain?

MARCH 5

You will continue to experience conflict if you do not gain specific Life Skills. Which ones do you need to improve?

1. Following directions
2. Listening
3. Apologizing
4. Focusing on tasks
5. Asking for help
6. Minding your own business
7. Asking for what you need
8. Accepting No for an answer
9. Asking permission
10. Resisting peer pressure
11. Completing undesirable tasks
12. Waiting
13. Accepting constructive criticism. This also falls under self-education, feedback avoidance, and measurement neglect.
14. Last but not least, working well with others. Which is the same thing you were rated for in kindergarten!
15. Are there any others that you can think of?

MARCH 6

Stop saying the word "like" in every sentence. It's a bad habit. Make it a goal to expand your vocabulary to sound more competent.

Use words like exemplary, affluent, cerebral, exquisite, witty, prolific, paramount, stalwart, immaculate, captivating, superb, deplorable, pragmatic, and ambivalent that equate the level of your education.

The number of syllables per page is referred to as 'Lexical.'

Eliminate the word "very" and click on synonyms to see alternatives to this word or the word that comes afterward.

What are your favorite words? You already know mine: **perspicacity**!

MARCH 7

People rarely mention this, but once you begin healing, your past traumas emerge out of the "fight, flight, freeze, fumble" choices that are part of the sympathetic nervous system response. Due to the release of trauma, your body requires much rest and sleep. Don't mistake the rest and sleep for depression. It isn't. Rest and sleep are essential because your body finally begins to feel safe and sound. Work through the sleepiness; it's temporary.

If you take it a day at a time through slow progress, it will add up to something monumental.

At this point in my life, the only person that I want to please is my higher power. If you have something in your heart, then it's there for a good reason.

Think of the negative self-talk as a big, negative giant named "Goliath." If you have negative self-talk, then bring awareness into the present, then code shift from the back brain perception to the front and then begin talking to your Spirit. The Present is all you have right now. This is also called Mindfulness.

How can you begin to throw some proactive words at your "Goliath"? Think about the 4 Bs of trauma: your body, your brain, your beliefs, and your behavior.

MARCH 8

When people get used to preferential treatment,
equal treatment feels like discrimination.
~Thomas Sowell~

A healthy person has a thousand wishes.
A sick person only has one.
~Indian proverb~

When a clown moves into a palace,
he doesn't become a king.
The palace becomes a circus.
~Turkish Proverb~

What does each quote mean to you?

MARCH 9

There is so much we can learn from the animal kingdom. I love biology, so I majored in it in college.

David Attenborough once shared that if you collect a hundred black ants and a hundred red ants and place them in a glass jar, they will live peacefully. But if you shake it violently and leave it on the table overnight, the ants will begin to fight with each other. The same is true for humans, whether it's man/woman, black/white, young/old, nation/country.

Before you begin fighting, inspect to see who shook the jar and how it happened.

The shaking of the jar is a metaphor for stirring the pot or knowingly or unknowingly creating a conflict that you did not have the *perspicacity* to foresee.

Sometimes, people send emails without thinking of the consequences of their haste. The speed at which people read their emails needs to slow down. The speed at which people react to those emails needs to slow down. It seems that people's priorities are to empty their email boxes as quickly as they can. This, undoubtedly, creates a mountain of conflict at work and in personal life. And, through texting too.

Slow down. Read. Respond. Don't react. Don't assume the worst. Don't put your feelings and emotions before your logic. Ask for clarification before you respond to an email.

There are no nonverbals in an email, which makes it rather difficult to ascertain the exact meaning coming from the sender.

Pick up the telephone. One phone call can eliminate seven emails. Did you know that? Yes!

Does this help? How?

MARCH 10

Neuroplasticity is the brain's ability to change itself by forming new neural connections in response to conditions and experiences. Traumatic Brain Injury is amazingly rectified in many cases through the beauty of neuroplasticity. This means that the brain is 'plastic' and not static.

You can promote Neuroplasticity by using your non-dominant hand to brush your teeth or to write, learning a new language or instrument, expanding your vocabulary, reading, writing, doing puzzles, drawing, singing, humming, drumming, meditating, walking backward, running, and exercising.

Did I say reading? If you read only 4% of your day, it will place you at the top of your field in ten years' time. Please find the time to read! Reading has the most bang for your buck.

Do you do any of the above activities? Which ones do you enjoy the most?

I believe that there are specialized neurons in the frontal lobe perception that can bring you *perspicacity*. It's those Aha moments when you 'get it'! I call these neurons "Neuro-sparks."

Perspicacity: The language and thinking about trauma are different from healing. Trauma says, "How could they betray me like that? What did I do to deserve that?" Healing says, "Their actions were their choice and had little to do with me. I can continue to focus on my healing and wellbeing."

How is trauma about perception?

MARCH 11

History is not there for you to judge. Although the brain loves to judge. It's not up to you to like it or dislike it. It's there for all of us to *learn* from it. If it offends you, then work on why things offend you so easily. We learn from our behavior history, so we don't repeat it!

It's not anyone's job to erase history. It belongs to all of us. We can all learn from it. My father told me that when the British invaded India, many Indians fled to other countries. It was the African Nations that took the Indians in. My father instructed me to help the African Nations, especially because of what the African Nations did for the Indians. Did you know that Mahatma Gandhi was educated and lived in Africa before going to India to save it from British rule?

What is your favorite time in history? Why? What did you learn from it?

MARCH 12

Personality is energy. Take responsibility for the energy you bring into every space. Our energy is a personality-driven by emotions.

From the bedroom to the bathroom, from the kitchen to the car, from the elevator to your desk at work, your personality changes. It's a fluid construction. Personality changes over time.

Some personalities will confront others, while others will ghost. Confronting is a sign of Fight, while ghosting is a sign of Flight.

Some things you can civilly say:

- I enjoyed getting to know you, but I don't feel a connection. Thank you for your time.
- This isn't working for me anymore. I hope you can understand.
- I have much going on in my life, and I'm not able to prioritize our relationship at this time.
- I don't want to work with you because I don't feel that you respect my boundaries.

Your attitude matters. Your words matter. Your participation matters. Your team matters. Take a slow and deep breath and make sure that your energy is positive and calm before entering those spaces today.

What kind of energy do you want to have at work? At home?

MARCH 13

Many mentally tough athletes discipline their internal dialogues. They are conscious that their thoughts dictate their behavior. They have learned to ignore doubt (self-doubt is the Impostor Phenomenon) through endless practice and planning, where practice makes perfect, and practice makes habit.

Say this to yourself:

I am winning financially.

I am winning physically.

I am winning, mentally.

I am winning at work.

I am winning in my personal life.

I am winning career-wise.

I am winning emotionally.

I am winning in my life.

I am winning because I am grateful.

Do you feel like you are winning? How?

MARCH 14

Pi day!

Go and treat yourself to your favorite piece of pie! Draw what it looked like here!

MARCH 15

How can you improve work culture through *values*?

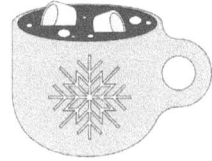

Reliability

Growth

Kindness

Mission/vision

Innovation

Transparency

Respect

Feedback

Collaboration AND Cooperation

Appreciation

Balance

Never assume anything. People do not share the same values. Communicate effectively and be transparent so people can understand exactly what you mean and to bring them onto the same page.

How do you communicate expectations at work and in your personal life?

MARCH 16

Whatever the present moment brings, accept it as if you had chosen it. The Present is all you have now.

Always work with things, not against them. This will miraculously transform your whole life. Eckhart Tolle

Nature loves courage. Be present. Accept and learn to take the No gracefully.

Why? Because when things go your way, the universe has your back. When things do not go your way, the universe *still* has your back! Understand this, and you will be much happier.

What will you do to arrive at Acceptance?

MARCH 17

The goal is not to pursue happiness because it is short-lived. The question is not, "How can I feel happier?" The question, through *perspicacity*, is, "How do I stop fueling my suffering?"

How are you bringing suffering into your life? Think about your thoughts, beliefs, words, and actions.

What can you do differently to alleviate the suffering that you are causing yourself?

MARCH 18

Your energy is a gift to this world—energy through extroversion, introversion, and ambiversion. The energy you bring is special and unique to you. This is powerful.

The world is inside of you. It is in your perception perspectives and your head-brain, gut-brain, and heart-brain.

To be happy, you must enjoy who you are. If you don't accept yourself, then how can others accept you?

Shine your energy and personality into this world. If it bothers someone, then let them cover their eyes!

Evolution can look like this:

Seeing people clearly without judging harshly.

Staying kind without getting close.

Maintaining boundaries without building walls.

Being aware without being affected.

Understanding without engaging.

How do you encourage others to shine?

MARCH 19

The Accountability Loop:

Recognize, self-examine, ownership, learn, forgive, learn.

The Victim Loop:

Ignore, deny, blame, rationalize, resist, avoid.

Which loop describes you? Why? Provide an example.

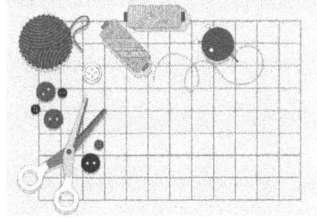

MARCH 20

That big goal in your heart is there for a distinct reason. Who you are, with the unique essence you have, is precisely what you need to actualize that goal.

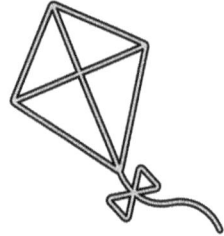

The fact that it's in your heart is not by accident. The universe has brought it to you and trusts you to carry it out for the sake of a peaceful world.

You can do this! You got this! Trust the flow.

What is your big vision for yourself? Your family? The world? How can you achieve it through *perspicacity*?

MARCH 21

Sound like a professional!

This literature review will critically examine the existing literature on...

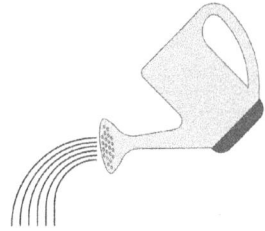

Contrary to the prevailing view in the literature, certain studies argue the opposite and have found that....

Critics argue that the existing frameworks in the literature oversimplify the following constructs....

Based on gaps identified in the literature, this study will address the following questions....

The literature suggests several answered questions that include the following...

There is much literature that highlights these points, and this presentation will expand upon this by....

Remember, people want Ethos, Logos, and Pathos, so be sure to include plenty of theories and studies that support what you are presenting to your audience.

What do you do when someone in the audience disagrees with you?

MARCH 22

Is Free Will an illusion? Do we genuinely have control over our actions, or are they just a reaction to the environment?

MARCH 23

Is morality objective, or is it subjective and culturally influenced?

MARCH 24

Can Artificial Intelligence attain true consciousness?

Why or why not?

MARCH 25

What is the nature of time? Is it a fundamental aspect of the universe or a human construct? How come you think you have all the time in the world?

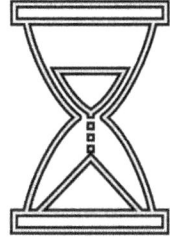

You have a survival mechanism that is rooted in your brain that wants you to survive and succeed. When I ask leaders why they want to be a leader of XYZ company, only 1 out of 10 can answer this question properly.

A sample answer: "I want to be a leader because I want to improve myself and improve NCDA. This is how I intend to improve myself…. This is how I intend to improve NCDA…"

Simple, accurate, and poised. When you are interviewing or being asked questions, be sure to state what you can bring to the table!!

How much time do you have to accomplish your ambitions? Why do you want to accomplish them so badly?

MARCH 26

Is the pursuit of happiness a worthwhile goal, or should you aim for something else?

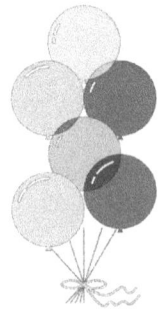

Why or why not?

MARCH 27

Many people are afraid of money. They are afraid of losing money. They are afraid they will not make as much as they spend. The thought of money, then, becomes a conditioning for fear, anxiety, and lack.

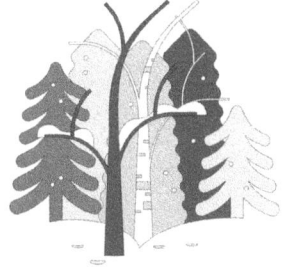

Money is a tool. Money is a mindset. Whatever you believe about money (or anything else for that matter) becomes your reality.

The four M's can help you learn to control your mind, mouth, mood, and money.

"Let me never fall into the vulgar mistake of dreaming that I am persecuted whenever I am contradicted."
~Ralph Waldo Emerson~

What does this quote mean to you?

How can you use this quote to gain **perspicacity**?

MARCH 28

Memory is *everything!* Without memory, you wouldn't have a life! Your entire existence is based on memory.

What is one positive childhood memory?

What is one positive adolescent memory? I specifically ask you this one because adolescents reject positive thinking. Many in this age group view it as naïve, and that causes them to reinforce their subconscious beliefs in the darkly negative form. Adolescents are fascinated by negativity because no one truly understands it.

What is one positive memory from school?

What is one positive memory from work?

Tell a negative memory, then code shift and tell the same story positively. How did that make you feel?

MARCH 29

Here are some good morning messages to begin your day (and emails).

Good morning

Wishing you sunshine

Have a blessed morning

Joyful day ahead

Embrace the day

Dream big today

New day, new possibilities

Positive vibes today

Enjoy today

Be amazing today

Sparkle

Shine

How do you radiate positivity at work and in your personal life?

MARCH 30

There is a condition called synesthesia, where people can see numbers in colors. Can you imagine how helpful that must be in doing math? The brain interprets signals from the eyes as light and sound from the ears, but a few people experience colors and sounds as smells, too.

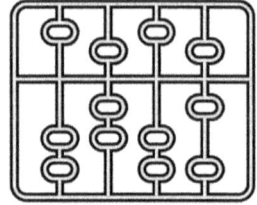

Have you ever thought about what colors taste like?

Would pink taste like cotton candy?

Would blue taste like shaved ice?

Would green taste like grass?

Would white taste like pudding?

Would orange taste like an orange?

Would purple taste like a grape?

MARCH 31

There is a condition called Alexithymia, which is the inability to identify, experience or express emotions verbally. Be kind to others because some people cannot detect emotions in other people.

Give grace to others. It's not you. It's not them. It's genetics.

Have you ever expressed your emotions to another only to have them stare at you? Describe the situation, how you felt, and what happened.

Knowing about Alexithymia, how would you react differently to that person?

Describe how responding through perspicacious intelligence is growth and maturity.

APRIL

APRIL 1

"Let us be thankful for the fools. But for them, the rest of us could not succeed."

~Mark Twain~

I think it's utterly foolish to judge people by the color of their skin. There's absolutely nothing they can do about the color of their skin. If you want to judge, then judge people by their character! The brain judges – it's just what it does, so be aware of HOW it judges at least.

Today is April Fool's Day, so everything that happens today is temporary. (Just like any other day).

When have you acted like a fool?

What lesson did you learn?

APRIL 2

Someone asked the landscaper why the plants grew so beautifully.

The guy answered: "I don't force them to grow this way. I just remove what stops them."

What miracle are you awaiting?

APRIL 3

If you are helping someone and expecting something in return, you are doing business, not kindness.

Altruism means that you will help another without asking for anything in return.

Birds, lions, and bears show altruism. Scientists have observed individual animals helping each other without asking anything in return.

Provide an example from the past where you helped someone and asked for something in return. How did that make you feel?

Can you help someone today without asking for anything in return?

APRIL 4

Your back brain perception is reactive and volatile. Your frontal lobe perception is responsive and logical. **Perspicacity** will tell you to pause if you are aware that it is your back brain perception in action.

You are really upset at what is happening because you judge that what is happening should be different from what is actually happening. Sometimes, your judgment is correct, but most of the time, it is not.

The best thing to do is to become aware and stop yourself in your tracks. Allow the emotion to pass. It takes time and patience for thoughts and feelings to move from the back brain perception to the frontal lobe perception. A different perspective will bring you some calm, but you must choose the calm because you have free will.

Write about an instance in the past where you did NOT pause. What was the outcome of the situation?

Write about an instance in the past where you paused. What was the outcome of the situation?

APRIL 5

All matter vibrates. Everything (your desk, chair, phone, pen, plate, purse, shirt...) is made up of matter, and all matter vibrates at different frequencies. It's physics. Atoms are in a constant state of motion, and depending on the speed of those atoms, things appear as solid, liquid, or gas. Sound is also a vibration, and so are thoughts.

Nothing rests. Everything moves. Everything vibrates. At the most fundamental level, the whole universe and everything that comprises it is pure vibratory energy that transforms itself in different ways. Matter is energy in a state of vibration.

You attract what vibrates at your same energy. What you think, say, and do will return back to you. If something is on your mind, it will physically appear.

The Law of Vibration states that everything in the universe vibrates at a specific frequency. Music, words, sound, and light all do.

How can you use the Law of Vibration to your advantage? Hint: You can surround yourself with positivity and raise your own vibration through words, music, sounds, and actions that bring you joy.

APRIL 6

Your natural state is one of fear and anxiety. The Amygdala in your back brain perception is in charge of that all day and night. You have to intentionally become aware of the emotions that keep you in low vibration.

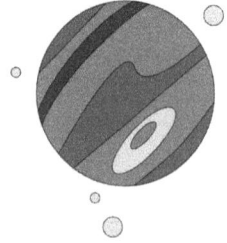

Breathing is one of the best things you can do for yourself. Deep breathing can help you to let go of fear and anxiety that floods your brain through the Sympathetic Nervous System. Release what holds you back there so you can focus on rising to a higher vibration. Worrying, anger, frustration, shame, and guilt all keep your vibration low. Breathe slowly through your nose so you can attain a higher vibration and also for your mind, body, and spirit.

Did you know that the universe has only one answer? And that answer is 'yes'. The universe will work with whatever you are thinking, feeling, and doing. If you say you are broke, the universe will say 'yes' and agree with you and bring more of that.

What you think is as powerful as what you utter.

What things do you need to release to increase your vibration? What things do you need to say to increase your vibration?

APRIL 7

You will never be able to solve your problems with the same mindset that caused your problems.

Nothing changes if nothing changes.

If you hold on to a grudge, good luck. If you burn bridges, good luck. If you like being somebody's follower, then good luck.

You will continue asking yourself, "Why is this happening to me?".

Months later, you will ask yourself, "Why is this happening to me AGAIN?"

You don't want change, but you want others to change and don't realize that it is YOU who must change.

Are you willing to let go of a grudge? Why or why not?

Are you willing to mend a bridge that you burned? Why or why not?

Are you willing to make decisions for yourself instead of following someone else's decision? (You're probably thinking that they will not be your friend if you disagree, and this is unhealthy).

APRIL 8

Free Will is real. Each day, you have a choice. You can either suffer mindlessly with bad habits, distractions, and vices, or you can improve purposefully through self-discipline. We're not talking about punishment here. Do not self-harm. We're talking about self-discipline, which means that you are adulting properly (maturely) through patience and empathy.

Back brain thinking: I deserve it more than them. I'm entitled to the promotion. Don't offend me or else.

Frontal Lobe thinking: I will challenge my thoughts because they may not be correct and might be there due to habitual thinking. No one owes me anything because I am responsible for my own success. It's okay if I didn't get the promotion and I will be glad for the person who got it.

The choice you make dictates whether you live a life of regret or a life of fulfillment. Suffering is unavoidable, but suffering for something worthwhile is a better choice. Choose wisely. Choose through *perspicacity*.

Are you self-disciplined? Why or why not?

APRIL 9

We all know what paranoia means, but do you know what **pronoia** is?

Pronoia is the belief that the universe is conspiring in your favor!

What are the benefits of having Pronoia versus paranoia?

Name an instance, one from work and one from home, where paranoia held you back.

Name an instance, one at work and one at home, where you will use Pronoia.

APRIL 10

Write about an experience that shaped your outlook on life.

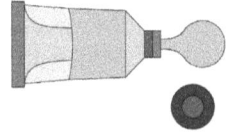

What is your worldview? To help you with this exercise, you can look at the lyrics of your favorite songs to learn what the singer's world view is. Singers often express their worldviews in their music as an expression of what they have seen or experienced. One of my favorite lyrics were written by superstar Neil Diamond. In his song "I am, I said. To no one there. No one heard me. Not even the chair.", he expresses his view of what is happening around him and how he felt at the time. Read these and see if you can feel his world view.

APRIL 11

Now that you know what **Perspicacity** is, list 3 beliefs that you can pivot to gain *perspicacity*. How will you pivot to bring about evidence of your *perspicacity*?

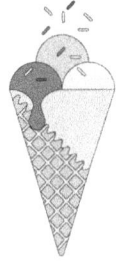

APRIL 12

Normally we give people permission to make mistakes and the obligation to learn from them. Some, however, just don't get it.

People who cannot communicate think everything is an argument. People who lack accountability think everything is an attack.

Learn to self-lead before you lead others. Otherwise, you will fail miserably.

It was General Colin Powell that said: "Great leaders are almost always great simplifiers who can cut through argument, debate, and doubt to offer solutions everyone can understand."

Can you tell me about a time you overcame a significant challenge at work? In your personal life?

APRIL 13

My family and I came here from India in search of the American Dream through hard-work and sacrifice, where the essence of who they were modeled gratitude and servitude to mankind.

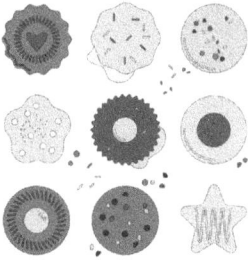

What is your American Dream?

How do you go about obtaining it?

APRIL 14

The book by Alexandre Dumas, "The Count of Monte Cristo," is one of my favorite books. The good guy wins!

"Scrooge" is my favorite Christmas book and movie. Both the book and the movie have psychological lessons regarding man's search for purpose and meaning.

What has been your most influential book(s) and movie(s)?

APRIL 15

Every workplace has some level of toxicity that includes cynicism, blame, and distrust.

We blame society. But aren't WE society?!

Listening for understanding is a key skill for any workplace.

Leaders who do not listen to their people will eventually be surrounded by people who have nothing to say. Such a workplace (or home) drains people. It they consistently feel depleted, then their peace is at stake and they will walk away.

Discuss 3 ways that a leader can listen to support individuals and teams better.

APRIL 16

My family reveres education.

Do you value education?

Make a sacrifice and be uncomfortable so a year or two so that you can be comfortable for the rest of your life.

What have you sacrificed in the name of education? Why?

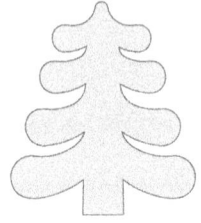

APRIL 17

It takes a long time to land a job and even longer to carve out a career that you are passionate about.

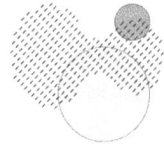

People rarely leave the work they love. Annoyed people leave people! Exasperated people leave systems!

Maybe the manager's leadership style doesn't work for them. Perhaps it's an annoying co-worker who does not share the same values. There could be several reasons, and it costs organizations plenty of time and money to rehire and retrain. Most companies rely on personality as a leadership style; some assume that extroverts make great leaders.

I did my post-doc work at a women's prison after I finished my dissertation, and it was the most gratifying work that I have ever done. My classes were filled to the max, and there was a one-year waiting list for them. I knew that I was doing "God's work" there. Prison culture is heavily system-based thinking, and it is truly an industrial complex, as author Irving Goffman puts it in his book "Total Institution." If we educate kids early enough, then it will not be necessary to punish grown men (Pythagoras). But alas, I digress.

What is one thing that you can do differently to understand and work with your manager? Co-workers? Foreign-born workers?

What are 3 things that you can do to help "justice-challenged" people?

APRIL 18

If you judge a fish by its ability to climb a tree, it will live its whole life believing that it is dumb.

It doesn't matter who is doing better. What matters is that you are using YOUR God-given skills, talents, and gifts to be an altruistic global citizen in this world.

Perspicacity: It really doesn't matter who is doing better than you as long as you're doing better than **you** did last year. It's always going to be you vs. you. The best thing you can do in this lifetime is to improve yourself.

Why do you compare yourself with others?

What can you do to gain a healthier sense of internal success?

APRIL 19

My **_perspicacity_** tells me to accept the fact that things did not happen the way I recall them.

If you are not aware, your back brain perception will insist that you stick to your story through cognitive dissonance. What is that? Cognitive Dissonance is when evidence that contradicts your beliefs is presented to you. This is everywhere, yet our brain refuses to accept another point of view.

Describe your perspective of an experience and how that point of view holds you back through your thinking and metacognition.

Discuss a story where you held on tightly to your belief. What happened when cognitive dissonance occurred?

What past experience do you find difficult to talk about, and why?

APRIL 20

When I think I'm unfairly hated,
I try to remember that I'm unfairly loved, too.
            ~R.C. Sproul~

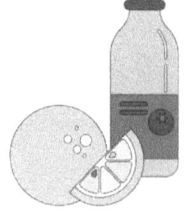

If you "Have," do not be arrogant towards those individuals or nations that "Do not Have."

Why do you think you have haters?

Perspicacity: feel the feelings but do not become the emotion. Witness, allow, and release. Read this twice.

APRIL 21

Silence is golden. New studies find that the more you vent the more you reinforce negativity. Learn to calm yourself, instead of venting to friends and family.

Have you ever sat in silence to seek the right answers? When? What happened?

Is there a favorite Podcast that can help you revel in calmness?

Perspicacity: Stay silent if you do not know the full story or if you feel unable to control your emotion or if you get angry or if you cannot talk without yelling. Anger just makes more work for you because you have to go back to the person and make things right again. Why not cultivate the self-discipline and lead yourself to respond correctly the first time?

APRIL 22

Don't be upset about the results you didn't get from the work you didn't do.

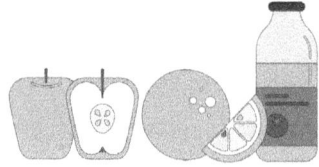

Let's get real today!

Proper preparation prevents poor performance. Asking for help is not a weakness. Ask for help.

Why are you hesitant to ask for help?

Think of a time when you asked for help. What happened?

APRIL 23

Forgiveness requires the **perspicacity** that someone's bad behavior is a sign of pain rather than wickedness.

Never tell a kid that they were a bad boy or girl. Do not focus on the person. Do not make it personal. Focus on behavior. It is the behavior that needs changing.

Your mistakes will introduce you to newer coping skills. For instance, have you tried EFT Tapping?

Never regret the kindness you show to someone who did not deserve it. They may have done you wrong, but you do not have to do wrong back to them.

What two things can you do to help yourself focus on the behavior and not on the person?

APRIL 24

The ego shouts. The Spirit whispers. Listen. Let it be.

Think words that mend the acrimony inside of you.

Speak words that rebuild the torn-down places in others. "Speaking words of wisdom, let it be," as the song goes.

The back irrational brain wants to get even. It wants others to suffer the same way they have made you suffer.

Growing up, adulting, and maturity requires **perspicacious** thinking. Feel those ill feelings and let them go rapidly without wallowing in pity.

Some people will judge you based on the color of your skin, but you do not have to do the same. We know that the brain loves to judge, so judge character. Character!

APRIL 25

Thank your higher power even before success happens!

We started praying for our sons-in-laws when our girls were in Kindergarten. We prayed that they were being raised in loving homes filled with peace, love, and understanding.

One day, they came into our lives! It happened!

Dear Higher Power, I'm thanking you even *before* it happens.

What are you praying for? Why?

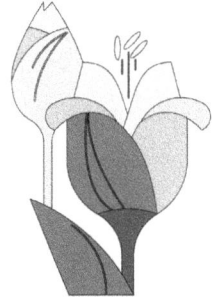

APRIL 26

You can continue to do your work as if it is a weight on your shoulders, or you can do it as if it is an opportunity to learn and grow towards **perspicacity**.

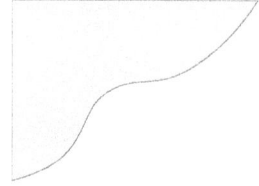

Celebrate their wins. You do not have to get jealous.

Try to remember the unique things about people you meet.

People do not hate their decent work; they hate being embarrassed, intimidated, and confused.

Empathy, understanding, and dialogue can yield unlocked treasure.

Make people feel safe by training your brain to become *nonjudgmental, impartial,* and *fair.*

APRIL 27

Perception can create a false sense of reality. Most people remain closed to hearing, seeking, and listening to the truth. Their reality will never be able to move their delusion.

I invite you to say these things if you do not want to burn a bridge:

- Let's agree to disagree since we have different points of view.
- It's difficult for me to engage with you when you speak with a harsh tone.
- It sounds like we are remembering things from a different perspective.
- My feelings are not invalid just because you disagree with them.
- I feel shocked when you dismiss what I am saying to you.
- I am open to brainstorming for solutions with you, but I am not open to debating how I feel.
- As I see it, both our feelings are equally valid.

There is not much you can do for the versions of you that exist in other people's minds. Culture + Values = radical loyalty to beliefs, assumptions, and bias!

Have you ever had your heart broken at work or in your personal life? What did you learn from that experience?

Discuss why we hang on to things that are not for us.

APRIL 28

Only speak what you wish to be brought into existence in your life.

What is your theme this year?

What 3 things will you do to stay focused on that theme?

APRIL 29

If nothing else, certain people just teach you how <u>not</u> to behave.

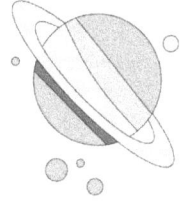

Think about the person you want to become. The voice of your spirit is as loud as your willingness to listen to it. Discernment can come to you, but hold the responsibility for your own Free Will to allow it to enter your head-heart-gut brains.

Your body needs good food, clean water, a roof over your head, positive energy, hormone awareness, proper sleep, and movement.

Your soul needs positivity, expressions, values, wisdom, knowledge, and connection.

Your spirit needs hope, acceptance, love, solitude, prayer, and peace.

Rene Descartes said: "We do not describe the world we see; we see the world we are able to describe."

What are my intentions for gaining *perspicacity* each month?

APRIL 30

It was Joan Didion that said this in her book "On Keeping A Notebook":

"I have already lost touch with a couple of people I used to be".

~~~~~~

You have distinct energy. It works for some contexts and not for others.

You have an attachment style. You struggle in your relationships because of a particular attachment style.

You have triggers and stressors for people, places, and things.

You have the tendency to self-sabotage. Do you fear success?

You have core beliefs. You have needs, wants, dreams, desires, and goals. Comprehend that everything that triggers you is seeking to transform you. The spirit is seeking to transform your entrapped perspectives and viewpoint. It wants to replace feelings and emotions with wisdom and perspicacity.

How will you allow the spirit inside of you to shine perspicaciously and intelligently?

MAY

MAY 1

Without trust, we don't truly collaborate,
we merely coordinate.
Trust transforms a bunch of people
into a team or a family.
~Stephen Covey~

Back brain perception: Because I carry guilt, I deserve punishment.

Frontal lobe perception: Code switch and write down a statement that does not sabotage you.

Back brain perception: Because I carry the blame, I should carry the burden for my whole family.

Frontal lobe perception: Use your metacognition to write an encouraging statement here.

Back brain perception: Because I am ashamed, I should hide away.

Frontal lobe perception: Use your ***perspicacity*** to write a promising statement here.

Learn to trust yourself before anything else. People cannot do what you do the way you do it. You are needed and valued in this world.

Perspicacity: Heal your wounds instead of spreading pain.

What aspects of yourself do you hide from others, and why?

MAY 2

> If you are not spiritually fed,
> then you will be emotionally led.
> ~Tara Bialek~

Many of us are aware that we use emotions to express how we feel but often fail to think about how Spirit can allow us to shape our lives wisely.

We know that the brain learns, so the capacity to learn is a gift, where the ability to learn is a skill, and the willingness to learn is a choice. Do you feel the *perspicacity* when you read my words?

How?

MAY 3

You must give love to get love.

Don't sit at home on the couch wishing and waiting for love. Show the world that you can give it, and it will surely come to you.

You will never find a perfect person. There is no such thing. The key is to decipher your values because everyone comes with things that they value. For example, if you value cleanliness and they don't, you two are not going to work out. If you value being on time and they are always late, it won't work. If you value talking, and they value silence, it won't work. If you value education and they don't, it won't work. If you value disruption and they value avoidance, it won't work.

Believe me! Trust me! I have conducted over two hundred mediations during my lifetime, and it always comes down to what people *value*.

Values are the key to ***perspicacity*** in work and life relationships.

Do you value wisdom, **perspicacity**, and intelligence?

MAY 4

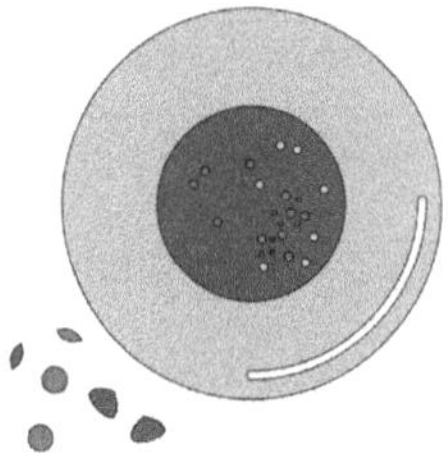

You have a handful of words that describe your Roles at work and in life.

Have you ever thought about being an Energy Converter?

Energy is like a currency. When you pay attention to something, you buy that experience. Your attention feeds the energy of what you focus on and keeps it alive inside your head, heart, and gut brains.

Perspicacity: If you do not like something, just take away its only power your attention.

How can you become an Energy Convertor at work and in your personal life?

MAY 5

It's Cinco de Mayo!

What 3 things would you like to celebrate today?

Shout out to every person who got through this
day without a nap. Ha! Actually, it's been proven that a power nap
can do wonders for you.

We're overworking, whether we are asked to or not.

We're overthinking whether we notice it or not.

Take a nap today!

Other than naps, what things are you doing for self-care?

MAY 6

Self-discovery and self-discipline are both imperative because they allow you to heal toward an optimistic worldview.

When you understand yourself better, you heal. When you understand why you do the things you do, you heal.

Allow your soul to accept the different narratives that you tell yourself so you can gain *perspicacity*. If you notice, when you are in your brain back, you tell yourself a certain story. When you are in your frontal lobe perception, there is a different story. Your story changes from your head, heart, and gut brains.

There are so many stories that you are telling yourself, and a different version to each person at each hour that approaches you. It can get chaotic inside the head brain.

Before you speak, allow your words to pass through a checklist. Is it true? Is it necessary? Is it kind?

Changing your stories may not guarantee that you will find *perspicacity*, but being negative will surely guarantee that you will not. As you change your stories, know that your beliefs and behavior will make your stories more positive.

Don't stop trying until you are proud of yourself.

MAY 7

Taichi Rule #1: never try to control anything outside of yourself. When you do, you are out of balance.

When a scale is balanced, there is no movement. If you put something on the scale, it will move until it is balanced, then it will stop again. So, balance is associated with movement and stillness. This balanced state is called "wuji."

When an outside force is applied to you, you feel out of balance. Rather than controlling that force, you can concentrate on what you need to do to go back to balance and stillness.

How can you restore your balance when something causes you to be imbalanced?

Train yourself to go from solitude and stillness to movement and back to solitude and stillness again.

What happened when you tried this?

MAY 8

The game of "Would you Rather."

Would you rather always speak your mind or never speak again?

Would you rather live in utopia as a commoner or be the ruler?

Would you rather go back in history or stay here?

Would you rather save your bank or all of your pictures?

Would you rather be able to control fire or water?

Would you rather go back to childhood or stay here at this age?

Would you rather have the ability to see ten minutes into the future or be invisible for ten minutes?

Let's talk about invisibility for a minute... There are invisible behaviors and those are: beliefs, values, metacognition, feelings, emotions. The visible are: behaviors, actions, and results.

MAY 9

Red flags never turn green.

You spend so much energy trying to change red flags that you fail to see the green flags.

Be careful who and what you invite into your soul.

How can you surrender to the spirit?

MAY 10

The Innocent achieves wisdom through too much trust and open-mindedness.

The Orphan, through cynicism and realism.

The Hero, through courage and helpfulness.

The Caregiver, through martyrdom and compassion.

The Rebel, through altering the norms of society through creativity and risk.

The Jester, through humor and pranks.

The Sage, through intelligence and insight. (This is me right now at my stage in lifespan development).

The Magician wants transformation through prestidigitation and distraction.

A ton of information is stored in your subconscious, but I want you to explore your consciousness. Which archetype are you? How do you try to achieve wisdom? It was Carl Jung that said: *"We cannot change anything until we accept it."*

MAY 11

Practice the pause. Sometimes, silence is golden.

Pause before judging.

Pause before assuming.

Pause before accusing.

Pause before reacting.

Pause blaming.

Pause shaming.

Wisdom is taking a pause.

Perspicacity: Being able to spot when your head is off your shoulders and needs redirection.

Describe a time when you used silence.

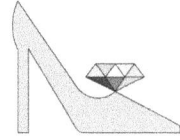

MAY 12

Give me a random piece of advice.

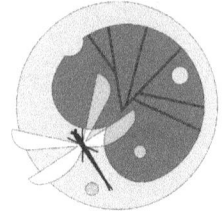

MAY 13

Awards that do not exist but you're always trying to win:

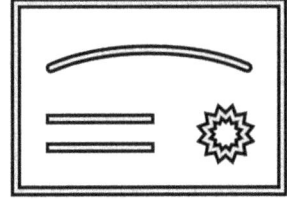

- Most perfect.

- Never said No.

- Didn't need help.

- Stayed late at work each night without overtime.

- Didn't make any mistakes.

- Lived up to everyone's expectations.

- Never called in sick.

- Did other people's work with a smile.

What award are you striving for? Why?

MAY 14

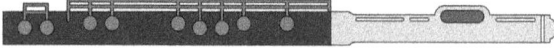

What is one thing that you've done that makes you fairly confident you're the only person who has done it?

What wisdom did you gain?

MAY 15

When you feel the urge to judge someone, judge that urge. This is *perspicacity*.

Contemplate where and when you have the urge to judge people. How can you change that behavior?

MAY 16

Key Performance Indicators are also known as KPIs. You use KPIs in the workplace.

Perspicacity: These are just as important in your personal life as they are in your job performance.

How do you keep people informed?

How do you keep people involved?

How do you keep people interested?

How do you keep people inspired?

MAY 17

Dr. Masaru Emoto is a Japanese researcher and author who found something groundbreaking regarding the nature of water (H_2O).

Emoto conducted an experiment where he labeled dishes of frozen water and observed the ice crystals that formed with positive and negative words and emotions.

The ones he labeled with negative words and emotions adversely affected the structure of the water, resulting in blurry and asymmetrical structures. In contrast, the dishes with positive words and emotions were clear and symmetrical.

He surmised that since the human body consists of 80% water, then positive and negative words would affect you, too.

He's correct in surmising this because words and emotions can be painful at the cellular level. At chronic levels, negativity can also cause somatic illness.

Your thoughts and emotions can change the molecular structure of water in your body!

How does negativity affect your body?

MAY 18

It's not that they don't like you. It's that immature people who know they've done you wrong will always distance themselves to avoid accountability.

People get jealous (back brain perception) of your shine. They don't stop to think about the time and effort it took you to get there.

Is accountability valuable to you? Why or why not?

Are you avoiding doing what is best for you? How can you conquer this resistance once and for all?

MAY 19

Your subconscious mind records everything. It's always alert and awake and controls 90% of your life. It's built on habits. It influences you during dreams and lives in your muscle memory.

It has no verbal language but interprets everything literally. It can do a billion things all at once. It is emotional, not logical.

Sometimes, you say something out loud, and you don't mean to say that; some people call it a Freudian slip of the tongue. Whether you meant it or not, your subconscious mind meant it and caused you to blurt.

Have you ever had a Freudian Slip of the tongue? What happened?

MAY 20

You may have a degree, but certain life skills are essential for you to learn.

How many of these do you know?

- ☐ How to write a proper email.
- ☐ How to write a thank-you letter.
- ☐ How to treat an older person.
- ☐ How to play with a baby.
- ☐ How to do laundry.
- ☐ How to sew a button on a shirt.
- ☐ How to run a vacuum and clean house.
- ☐ How to hammer in a nail and fix something instead of replacing it.
- ☐ How to shake hands.
- ☐ How to introduce yourself and what you do.
- ☐ How to boil water, read a recipe, or make scrambled eggs.
- ☐ How to balance your finances on an Excel spreadsheet.
- ☐ How to take care of plants and animals.
- ☐ How to wash dishes.
- ☐ How to make a budget.
- ☐ How to check tire pressure.

- [ ] How to apologize.

- [ ] How to get along with other cultures.

- [ ] How to eat with your mouth closed and other restaurant manners.

- [ ] How to manage anger.

- [ ] How to be an adult and live by yourself without your parents.

MAY 21

Since birth, your brain has been learning. So far, you have accepted the worldview that has been embedded in you through conditioning.

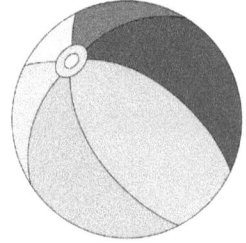

At some point in lifespan development, you will reject your parents' beliefs and views. At some point, usually in adolescence, you will sense that something is missing in your life, and you will begin to look for answers outside of your immediate circle.

Your inner Spirit will lead and awaken you and show you different cultures and perspectives of the world, and this will lend to your *perspicacity*.

Live beneath your means.

Stop blaming other people.

Return borrowed things.

Admit it when you make a mistake.

Give clothes to charity.

Listen more.

Be early, because when you're on time, you're late.

Be humble.

Don't sweat the small stuff because it's all small stuff. (Read the book; it's a good one!). I believe that you will sweat less when you replace perception with perspective. Perspectives lead to collaboration, because when you are open to other ideas and believe that those ideas will benefit everyone, well then, isn't that wisdom?

What is one belief that your parents hold that you do not? Why?

MAY 22

All human beings are descendants of tribal people who were spiritually alive and intimately in love with nature and the Earth. As tribal people, we knew who we were, we knew where we were, and we knew our purpose. This sacred perception of reality remains alive and well in our genetic memory. We carry it inside of us in our DNA.

The solitary individual has always had to struggle to keep from being overwhelmed by the tribe. If you try it, you will be lonely and frightened. But no price is too high to pay for the honor of being true to yourself.

~John Trudell~

Struggle means that you are being shaped for something bigger.

Pain means there is something you need to let go. Let me put it another way—letting go means to accept what is already gone.

Rejection means this was not meant for you.

Loss means you are learning to appreciate what matters.

Hardships help you build strength. Try a strength-based approach.

Uncertainty means there will be possibilities.

What is your sacred perception of life?

MAY 23

Two truths can coexist.

You can have hard conversations
and stay safe for each other.

You can be friends and still get annoyed at each other.

Wisdom: If you become friends with yourself, you will never feel alone.

You can enjoy each other's company and want to be by yourself.

You can appreciate what they are doing and request a change.

You can be upset and still be kind.

You can be busy and still be available for someone.

You can appreciate the effort and still have unmet needs.

You can feel triggered and still remain calm and collected.

The best decision I ever made was...

MAY 24

Christopher Walken, an actor, once said that no one is leaving this Earth alive, so eat delicious food, take long walks, jump in the water, be silly, be weird, and speak the truth that you are carrying in your heart like a hidden treasure because there is no time for anything else.

The soul has no secrets that your behavior will not reveal in time.

I have traveled through madness to find myself because....

MAY 25

Your oddness is probably your greatest asset.

What are two of your eccentricities, and how can you appreciate them?

MAY 26

It's a beautiful day, and you can't see it.

The egoic mind thrives on the illusion of control. Strength emerges when you surrender the need to dictate outcomes and flow with the unfolding reality around you.

The higher you are placed. The more humbly you need to walk because when you choose the behavior, you choose your consequences.

MAY 27

Truth does not mind being questioned.

A lie does not like being challenged.

Was there a situation where you squirmed, to tell the truth? Why? What happened?

MAY 28

You become unhappy because you are not in sync with who you are and not because of what anyone else is doing or not doing.

Remember, you are the only person on Earth that can make you happy. Happiness comes from within, not without, where the only thing that makes you unhappy are your own thoughts and thinking those thoughts over and over again.

You are an intelligent person with a heart. How can you bring your head-heart-gut brain to synchronize with each other?

What is one thing that you have not told anyone? Why have you kept this a secret?

MAY 29

When you complain about something, you make
yourself a victim. It doesn't matter if it's through
a phone call, text, email, Facebook, Instagram, or
LinkedIn.

Either accept the situation or leave it behind. All else is maddening.

Don't get mad at the other person because you wrote to them. You
have no control over their reaction. They react through their unique
schema.

Describe a time when you complained to another person.

What happened? What can you do differently next time?

MAY 30

Compliments you can give yourself!

- You're inspiring.
- You have great ideas. Ideas are what motivate you and cause you to create joyful goals. How can you become the type of person who deserves the life you are imagining?
- You're smart. In different ways than others.
- You're talented. In different ways than others.

Compliment yourself and others!

MAY 31

Many times, there is an elephant in the room. Not literally, but figuratively. It means that there is a topic that everyone is thinking about, yet no one mentions. No one acknowledges it.

If we do not acknowledge the things which make us afraid, then how will we think critically?

A great example of not saying what you need to say is the Borders bookstore that went out of business. The CEO refused to believe in digital books. The topic became an elephant in the boardroom.

The perspicacity here is that the choices you make will define you much more than your circumstances ever will.

What is the elephant in your room that you are afraid to address?

JUNE

JUNE 1

Don't judge someone or something just because they sin differently than you.

Everyone falls short at one time or another. Nine-tenths of work and life is about attitudes and self-talk.

How do you pivot when your thoughts spiral downward?

Where and when do you need the most encouragement? Why?

JUNE 2

Colin Powell believed that great leaders simplifiers of complicated information.

They can cut through debates, arguments, and doubts by brainstorming solutions that everyone can understand.

How are you showing up in the world?

I have portrayed myself in this manner on LinkedIn. This is who I am and where I want to go at this point in my lifespan stage.

Look at your LinkedIn profile. Does it state who you are, where you're going, and how you intend to get there?

Write it here.

JUNE 3

Was it really a bad day, or did you have 30 minutes when your thoughts fell into your back, your irrational brain, and your emotional center?

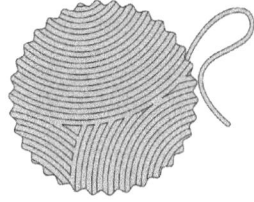

Where and when did this happen?

How many times a month does this happen?

Why do you need to learn how to self-lead?

JUNE 4

Everything you hear is an opinion and not a fact. Everything you see is a perspective and not the truth.

~Marcus Aurelis~

Don't cling to a mistake just because you spend years making it.

How can you reset?

JUNE 5

Everyone is out there trying to find love.

Your task is not too long for or wish for love but to seek and find all the barriers within yourself that you have built against love.

~Rumi~

Longing, wishing, and dreaming do not take away worry; they only take away today's peace of mind.

How can you spend your time productively and positively?

JUNE 6

How easily triggered are you? Why? Where and when do you get triggered the most?

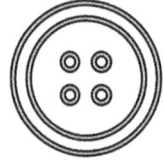

Do the following things bother you? Why?

Pineapple on pizza.

Books are better than movies.

Dogs are smarter than cats.

Video games are art.

Social media does not harm.

Be a vegetarian.

Tea is much better than coffee.

Half the population does not know how to swim.

Online relationships are just as meaningful as in-person ones.

We don't need physical books.

Reality TV should replace everything else.

All schools should be virtual. Turn the school buildings into housing for the poor.

JUNE 7

Have you ever eaten something that was expired?

Have you ever forgotten someone's birthday?

Have you ever scrolled through someone else's phone?

Have you ever walked into a glass door?

Have you ever forgotten your wallet or purse at home?

Have you ever been to another country?

Have you tried ethnic foods?

Have you ever walked out of a bathroom with tissue on your shoe?

Have you ever slipped and fallen on a banana peel?

Have you ever slept through your alarm?

Have you ever had a bird poop on you?

Have you ever forgotten someone's name while talking to them?

Find the *perspicacity* in each one of these above!

JUNE 8

> *"The problem is not the problem.*
> *The problem is your attitude*
> *about the problem."*
>
> ~Jack Sparrow~

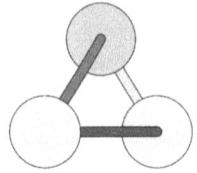

How can you fix your attitude?

Describe a situation when you had a poor attitude.

What happened? Where & When? How would you do things differently?

JUNE 9

A variety of species exists in the animal kingdom. A fish knows how to swim. A rhinoceros puts out campfires. Monkeys can make tools to get food. By the same token, you (biological name - Homo Sapien) have a distinct brain, abilities, and skills.

How do you utilize the skills of your colleagues in conjunction with yours?

Make a list of 4 skills that are necessary at work. At home?

JUNE 10

Elements of Critical Thinking.

Clarification helps you understand a problem.

Accuracy makes sure that the information you use is correct.

Language helps you to be specific without confusion.

Relevance brings you to focus on what truly matters.

Logic creates logical reasoning to evaluate arguments and reach valid conclusions.

Fairness allows an open mind. But a word here from me is that this depends on context. I believe that it's not fair to treat all of your children the same. Why? Because each has a different personality and needs. Get this!

Impartiality is not to take sides. Present the facts. Brainstorm. Choose a viable solution. Extra credit: read the story of King Solomon, who advised two women who claimed a baby was theirs.

Nonjudgmental means that you do not judge based on *your* beliefs, assumptions, biases, and schema.

Which one (s) do you need to improve upon, and how will you improve those?

The Tao Te Ching of China talks much about fulfillment. How do you find fulfillment?

JUNE 11

There is no perfect day or time to do something you want to do. If doing the thing makes you feel right, then go for it. You don't have to wait for the right conditions or the right day to begin.

Use the resources you have right now, today. Take the first step on the ladder without looking at the tall length of it.

What is it that you want to go for? Why do you want it so badly?

What is the difference between Living and Existing?

JUNE 12

My life changed when I realized that people were not intentionally trying to hurt me.

People are just trying to keep themselves safe in the ways that they know how.

Acceptance shows up in various languages beyond words. Those languages are just as valid to the person positioning or behaving that way.

The judgment you have for others directly reflects the areas where you judge yourself.

The acceptance you have for others directly reflects the acceptance you have for yourself.

What is the career and life story that you are telling yourself? Why do you choose those words to describe your story? Are there different words that you can use?

JUNE 13

How do you feel today, and why?

I feel left out and excluded.

I feel powerless.

I feel judged.

I feel unheard.

I feel blamed.

I feel trapped.

I feel scared.

I feel embarrassed.

I feel unsafe.

I feel lonely.

I feel unloved.

I feel ashamed.

I feel guilty.

I feel manipulated.

I feel disappointed.

Know that all of these feelings are just descriptions that your brain has conjured up. They are an implication that you are disconnected from those around you, and it happens when you depend on interaction to understand and accept yourself. That interaction has little to do with how other people treat you and much more to do with how you perceive yourself based on how others treat you. Get it?

JUNE 14

Pleasure cannot cure your pain. Both come from the Limbic System in your mid-brain. Pleasure is not about how great you feel but rather *why* you feel it. People who live immorally feel just as happy as people who have morals. Use pain to serve you and employ it as a guiding force for what you believe is good instead of working against it. Remember, every relationship that you have with a person, place, or thing is the one you have with yourself.

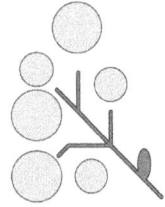

I assume evil intent because...

I do not assume evil intent because...

JUNE 15

"Often when you think that you are at the end of something, you are at the beginning of something else."

~Mr. Rodgers~

What are you ending? What are you beginning?

JUNE 16

I resolve internal conflicts by...

I resolve external conflicts by...

JUNE 17

What are two things you want your partner (if you don't have a life partner, then your best friend or family member) to know?

JUNE 18

Where in the world do you want to travel?

Why?

JUNE 19

"Accept the moment.
Whatever the present moment contains,
accept it as if you had chosen it.
Work with it, not against it.
This will help you to transform your whole life."
~Eckhart Tolle~

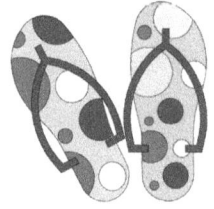

How can you stop fighting with your life?

JUNE 20

Write a letter to your enemy.

Begin every sentence with the word "Green."

Describe how you are your own worst enemy.

What did you learn from this exercise?

JUNE 21

What is your favorite song?

Write down the lyrics.

Why do those lyrics resonate so deeply with you?

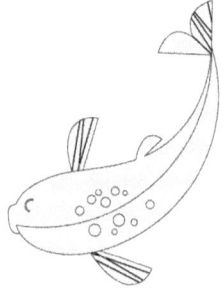

JUNE 22

Draw yourself.

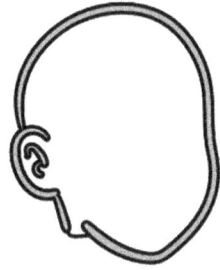

JUNE 23

A 600-pound life can be either through biology (weight), psychology (emotions), social (people), or the culture (traditions) of you.

The only way out is to go through the thing (Robert Frost).

Do you carry biological, psychological, social, or cultural weight? Why?

JUNE 24

Lessons people learn too late in life. What lessons do you need to learn?

Self-acceptance.

Setting boundaries.

Prioritizing their needs.

Distinguishing between needs and wants.

Financial literacy.

Embracing aging.

Letting go of perfection.

Using emotional intelligence.

Resilience.

Evaluating priorities.

Pivoting.

Resetting.

Appreciating the present moment.

Letting go of regrets.

Understanding cultures.

JUNE 25

Do you know what Active listening is? How do you feel when someone is giving you their total and undivided attention? Active listening requires that you listen to understand and not to listen to reply.

Most people have not had their voices heard in the way they want. When someone listens to you, healing occurs. When you listen to others through loving curiosity, it is a gift to them.

How do you listen to others? Why is it so important?

JUNE 26

Rules for being human from ancient Sanskrit.

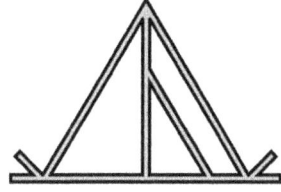

1. You will receive a body.
2. You will learn lessons.
3. That lesson will be repeated until you learn it.
4. "There" is no better than "here."
5. Other people are mirrors of you.
6. What you make of your life is up to you. Failure precedes success.
7. Life will be exactly what you think of it. Thinking and doing are two different things.
8. The answers are inside of you. You are too busy looking outward and that is not productive time spent.

JUNE 27

The most dangerous sentence in any language is, "We have always done it this way.".

When you open up to others, you become magnetic. The secret to becoming more magnetic is openness. Free yourself from your thinking and dissolve limitations (and the neuroticism in the emotional brain) that have blocked your openness.

When you are open to receiving, you become magnetic, and you inspire and empower others without effort.

What do you need to become more magnetic?

JUNE 28

The whole department will take on the personality of their leader. If the leader is mean, then the department will be mean to one another.

If the leader is open to receiving, then the department will also be the same.

The leader can either extinguish a positive flame or ignite that flame of hope.

The leader is responsible for the culture, mood, and outcomes of their department. Ultimately, the leader will have to take responsibility for their actions and how they are self-leading and leading their team.

What do you want to say to your boss? What do you want to tell your leader?

JUNE 29

The Dunning-Kruger Effect is a cognitive bias in which people with low levels of skill mistakenly believe they possess.

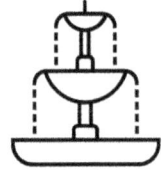

This overestimation stems from insufficient self-awareness regarding their knowledge gaps.

Where have you seen this effect?

JUNE 30

You are entirely up to you.

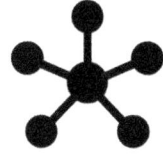

You are who you are due to your bias! Explore your biases every day. Ask yourself: do you consistently seek information that supports your way of thinking, your beliefs, or your memory? What is your Bias?

Confirmation Bias is listening more often to information that confirms your existing beliefs. You favor information that reinforces what you believe and dismiss other evidence that says otherwise.

Halo Effect is the tendency for the initial impression of a person to influence what you think of them overall.

Hindsight Bias is the tendency to see events, even random ones, as more predictable than they are. It is also commonly referred to as the "I knew it all along" phenomenon.

Anchoring Bias is the tendency to rely on and be influenced by the first piece of information obtained and use it as a baseline for comparisons.

Bandwagon Effect is deciding based on what others believe in. Similar to Groupthink and Heard Mentality. Groupthink is a term uses by Irving Janis and it happens when a group makes a faulty decision because they ignore alternatives and when there are no clear rules for decision-making. Please Google the heart-wrenching story of Kitty Genovese.

Be careful when you are in a group. Don't get swept up with the crowd. When you are young it's called 'peer pressure' and when you are an adult it's called 'groupthink'. In order to be accepted, people unwittingly mirror behaviors when they are in a group setting.

Self-serving Bias is the tendency to give ourselves credit for successes but lay blame for the failures on external causes. External attribution.

MID-YEAR WISDOM

How can you tell if you have the gift of perspicacity?

You listen to people's feelings through their dialogues and narratives.

You observe, more than you speak.

You do not assume; you ask clarifying questions.

You sense the importance of certain things.

You spend time with the spirit.

You know how to inspire yourself and others.

Naisei, in Japanese, is Introspection. Looking inward to develop self-awareness and examining one's thoughts, feelings, and actions. The culture values listening, quietness, and peacefulness.

Itadakimasu, in Japanese, means "I humbly receive." The culture understands and values wisdom. When you humble yourself and are open to receiving new information, your metacognition will shift.

Mushkin, a Zen practice, is when your mind is completely free and present. The culture understands the importance of living in the present without regrets from the past interfering.

Ikigai, a Japanese belief, says to take things slower and reconnect with nature.

As you get closer to nature, you connect deeper with the spirit. Physics is where they hide scientific proof of spirituality. You believe in gravity, even though you cannot see it. You feel it in action each time you drop something on the ground. By the same token, there are forces and laws in motion that you cannot see. Trust and believe they exist.

Consider how precious your spirit must be if both God and the Devil want it. Ubuntu, an African concept, says that you will make mistakes, but your soul is still good despite this fact. YOU are entirely up to you. It is never too late because God does not use the same clock as you. So, before you think otherwise, let your words pass through two truths: Is it true? Is it kind?

The Wise Mind is a mindful, intuitive, rational, and balanced mind. As badly as you wish to address certain things, it is wiser to leave certain things alone. Allow the universe to make things straight. Your brain will choose familiar chaos over unfamiliar peace. You cannot borrow preparedness from someone else.

There are counter-intuitive lessons that are wise.

1. Trying too hard to impress will make them walk away.
2. Learn to be alone, before you take on another person's life.
3. The more knowledge you gain, the more you will feel as though you do not know anything.
4. The more you take responsibility for your mistakes, the more people will respect you.
5. When you point out an ill trait in someone else, you are that way yourself and that's why you recognize it.

Find people who do not live in fear. Those that are magnetic, vibrant, and create magic in this world. Quality is never an accident. It is always the result of high intention, effort, and skillful direction.

The Laws of Detachment:

1. Allow others to be who they are.
2. Allow yourself to be who you are.

3. Uncertainty is reality.
4. Don't force situations.
5. Solutions naturally emerge

There are five types of Rest:

1. Physical: It is wise to take that nap.
2. Emotional: It is wise to keep a journal.
3. Sensory: It is wise to take a break from the screen.
4. Social: It is wise to take a break from people.
5. Spiritual: It is wise to make the time to reflect and evaluate.

Transform information into wisdom.

1. Deconstruct – break down complex information into smaller chunks to make it manageable.
2. Reconstruct – build that information back up in your own words.
3. Connection – link it to something you already know.
4. Challenge – contest your thinking and come up with another perspective.
5. Apply – explain what you learned, especially the wisdom you found in that information.

Knowledge is a powerful thing. No one can take it away from you. The key is to use it wisely.

That's Not My Job! Everybody, Somebody, Anybody, and Nobody go to work every day. There was an important job to be done, and Everybody was sure that Somebody would do it. Anybody could have done it, but Nobody did it. Somebody got angry about that because it was Everybody's job. Everybody thought Anybody could do it, but Nobody realized that Everybody wouldn't do it. It ended up that Everybody blamed Somebody when Nobody did what Anybody could have done.

Wise One-Liners:

1. You can be mad, but you shouldn't be mean.
2. It is perfectly acceptable not to be okay for a minute.
3. Do you want me to talk or just listen?
4. Every family has different rules.
5. Don't put down someone's yummy.
6. You can be kind without being best friends.
7. Don't gossip or tattle to get someone in trouble. Karma will find you.

Your brain was made to sense, perceive, judge, and think, while your gut-brain was made to be intuitive. You have been given the gift of Free Will. You can use it by disciplining yourself to have control over several parts of your brain. Instead of judging and over thinking, you can do more observing, listening, and loving. This is much more perspicacious. Are you feeling wiser yet? Do you have the wisdom to know the difference yet?

JULY

JULY 1

Key Performance Indicators.

Keep people interested.

Keep people informed.

Keep people involved.

Keep people inspired.

How?

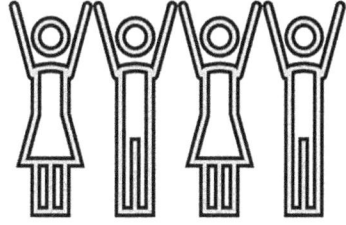

JULY 2

The capacity to learn is a gift.

The ability to learn is a skill.

The willingness to learn is a choice.

What 3 things do you still need to learn?

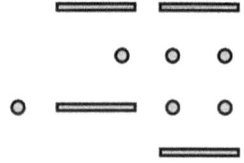

JULY 3

What are 2 things that bring you joy? Why?

The **Wise Mind** maintains harmony between the rational and emotional regions of the brain. It acknowledges and responds to others' feelings while still responding to them logically.

The **Emotional Mind** controls a person's feelings and dismisses logic. It makes impulsive decisions with little thought for the consequences.

The **Rational Mind** approaches life rationally, employing reason and logic in the thinking process and the information available. It is a grateful mind that sees lessons and opportunities. It is an abundance mindset that takes accountability to create a different reality.

The **Ego Mind** sees only mistakes and complains about everything. This is a scarcity mindset that lives in a victim mentality. The perspicacity here is for you to spend more time with groups who are helping your soul; not your ego.

JULY 4

Why do you love your country so much?

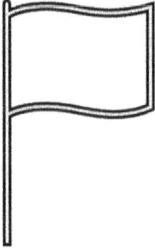

JULY 5

How do you connect with your community?

Why is it important to connect with your community?

JULY 6

Should Artificial Intelligence have rights?

Why or why not?

JULY 7

Fasting from people is just as important as fasting from food.

What people do you need to fast from? Why?

What are you physically and mentally consuming? Why?

JULY 8

Carl Jung did 'Shadow Work' with his clients. Have you done the Shadow Work within you?

Shadow work is the term coined by Carl Jung who states that it is the wise mind that accepts that there is internal strife that needs to be addressed and resolved.

Have you done the Shadow Work within you?

Is there anything you are insecure about?

When and where do you feel fear and anxiety?

What are your best and worst qualities?

Who are you jealous of?

What things hold you back?

What do you need to let go of?

What else do you want to achieve in life?

What emotions do you try to hide?

What needs forgiveness?

What is wisdom?

JULY 9

Parkinson's Law states that if you have all day long to do a task, it will take you the whole day, but if you only have two hours to do that task, then you will find a way to complete it in two hours.

Where are you in your lifespan development?

How much time do you have left to make a difference in this world?

Do you know what you are doing with your life? How?

JULY 10

There are evidence-based constructions that can surely help you gain wisdom, but wisdom can also bring pain.

Lamborghini was a tractor company. Samsung was a grocery store. LG was a facial cream, while IKEA was a pen. There is a lesson here! Everything is temporary, and your current situation is not your last. Keep at it and stay humble when success comes through the door!

If you truly want to be wise, then you must master your feelings and emotions during painful (laborious) times.

At first, you will have much motivation, but as situations arise, the motivation will wane a bit, and this is because you have equated progress solely to things that go your way.

What you need is perseverance through the times when things do not go your way because those are the times of great learning lessons.

Wisdom is gained through desire, time, and self-discipline.

Describe a time when wisdom was painful. What happened?

JULY 11

Every day that you live, you are presented with choices. You have the choice to evolve or remain as you are, with your heels embedded stubbornly in the sand.

If you choose to remain as you are, you will be presented with life lessons repeatedly until you learn to change.

You will ask yourself, "Why is this happening to me? Why is this happening to me again?".

To become a better version of yourself, it takes inspection of the self; it takes introspection to admit the negatives.

You have been given everything you need to live the life you have. It's up to you to evolve or remain as you are.

Carl Jung said: "You are what you do, not what you say you'll do."

What is the **perspicacity** here?

JULY 12

Who do you need to apologize to?

You can do it this way if you want.

1. Express regret.
2. Accept your part.
3. Make amends.
4. Repent.
5. Request forgiveness.

JULY 13

Things bother you because you are not the center of attention, and you're not getting what you want.

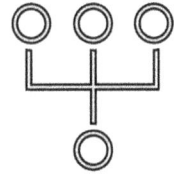

Your ego wants recognition and nomination much of the time because you see things only from your lens. You must learn to let go of old ways if they don't work out. Evolve into a conscious person who is inclusive and elevates others, not solely yourself. Let others recognize you without manipulation. If you listen to your ego, you may end up forsaking valuable connections and being surrounded solely by those who idolize you.

What things make you feel powerless? Why?

Your story is not finished yet. You will laugh at the places where you cried. Keep making progress. Your Spirit is with you and guiding you.

JULY 14

The four cardinal virtues of stoicism are:

Wisdom, courage, justice, and self-control.

Seek knowledge. Cultivate rationality. Do not judge.

Think through reason. Strive for self-improvement.

Face the world through resilience and bravery. Act through your values.

Treat others as you wish to be treated.

Treat others through kindness and empathy.

Practice self-control. Avoid excess.

Maintain a balance between your desires, needs, and wants.

Which ones are you working on?

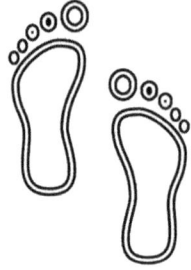

JULY 15

Allow people to be who they are.

Decide if you want them in your life.

Trust that rejection is a redirection to something better.

Certain people are only meant to help you grow and not be in your life forever.

How is everything that is falling apart transitioning into a different and improved state?

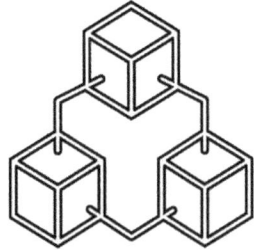

JULY 16

Signs that your brain is on autopilot.

Doing things without thinking. Zoning out.

Struggling with details. Passive with goals.

Most days lack meaning or purpose.

You say yes to things you don't want to do because you are unsure of your own needs.

You feel overwhelmed. You feel disconnected.

You purposefully fill your day with mindless activities to pass the time.

You dread tomorrow because there is nothing to look forward to.

Is there someone you can talk to about your feelings and emotions?

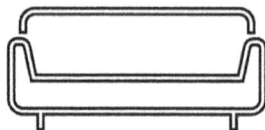

JULY 17

How to stay unbothered.

Don't worry too much about what others say.

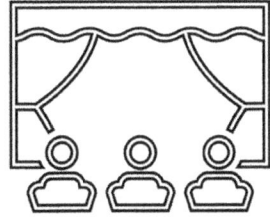

You don't need to explain yourself.

Do not allow your emotions to lead.

Your flaws make you who you are. Either accept them or change.

Expect nothing, and you will not be disappointed.

Know your values.

Set limits. Set boundaries.

You cannot please everyone because there are far too many opinions. In the end, you have to decide for your good and/or for the good of all.

Focus on helping this world, not on showing off to the world.

You feel like you need to show off because there is much competition in this world, and that is how you were conditioned. What can you do about the side of you that wants to show off?

JULY 18

There are many ways to increase your intelligence.

Howard Gardner researched multiple intelligences, and his research found that people can be good at a myriad of things and not just be book-smart. There is math, art, physical, spiritual, science, spatial, nature, and other intelligences where people can show their innate talents.

You can increase your intelligence by:

Reading on a variety of subjects and disciplines.

Increasing the diversity of meanings, interpretations, and perspectives.

Participating in physical movement.

Defying conventional labels and norms.

Having a great circle of influencers.

Find culturally different ways of doing things.

How are you improving your intelligence?

You're coaching leaders from miscellaneous cultures.

How can you adjust cultural intelligence to connect effectively?

JULY 19

The best way to gain wisdom is to triple your failure rate.

Agree or disagree? Why or why not?

JULY 20

Your nervous system will always choose familiar chaos over unfamiliar peace until you learn to heal and choose differently.

Sometimes, it feels much better not to talk. Agree or disagree? Why?

JULY 21

You are not a grown-up until you know how to communicate in your culture as well as with other cultures.

How do you interact with other cultures? Is it working for you? Why or why not?

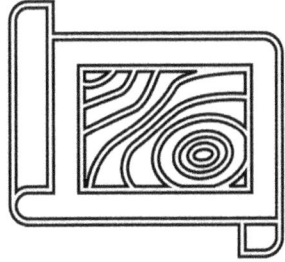

JULY 22

Four Agreements.

Be impeccable with your word. Say what you mean and mean what you say.

Don't take anything personally. Not everything is about you. They're not being, doing, or saying because of you. What others say and do is a projection of their reality and perceptions. Make yourself immune to the opinions and actions of others. Observe, don't absorb.

Don't make assumptions. Ask good questions to get clarification. Take a step back from those who misunderstand you through drama and don't want to understand.

Always do your best. Always bring your best self to the table. Compartmentalize your feelings and emotions and begin fresh at each meeting.

Which one do you need to work on? Why?

JULY 23

You can forgive people without welcoming them back into your life. Apology accepted.

Access denied. Who knows? Maybe things will change in the future.

Who are you denying access to? Why?

JULY 24

Don't forget how badly you once wanted what you have now!

What things are you thankful for?

What relationships are you grateful for?

How are you maintaining peace, love, and understanding in your life?

JULY 25

Money is a tool.

What does it take to blow ten thousand dollars a year?

Only $27.40 per day.

Where is your money going?

What kind of relationship do you have with money?

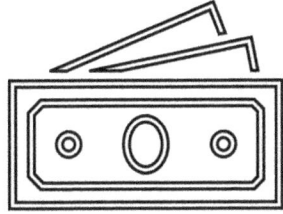

JULY 26

What books are you reading?

1. Flow
2. Learned Optimism
3. Mindset
4. The Count of Monte Cristo
5. Scrooge
6. Activate Success, Tips, Tools, & Insights to Be a Leader in Your Niche

Why is it important to read good books? I'll share my answer and then you can write yours.

It's important to read books because the person you will be next year depends on it, because the purpose of knowledge is wisdom.

JULY 27

I just feel like I need to lie down for a few years.

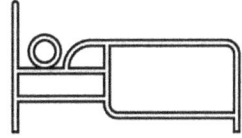

Many cultures promote short power naps. What is the benefit of napping?

Do you feel more productive after a good nap? Is napping a form of self-care? Why or why not?

What other self-care behaviors do you engage in?

JULY 28

"Quality is never an accident.

It is always the result of high intention, good effort, and intelligent direction with skillful execution.

It represents the wise choice of many alternatives."

~Willis A. Foster~

Your thoughts?

JULY 29

Labels.

A goal without a deadline is just a fantasy.

A goal with a deadline is an objective.

A goal plus a deadline and plan equals success.

A goal with consistent action equals success.

A goal that is meaningful equals fulfillment.

I will tell you that the happier you are with a decision, the less you will need others to be happy or even need validation from another.

If you were forced to wear a warning label, what would yours say?

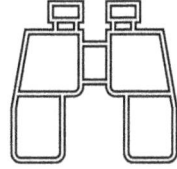

JULY 30

Have you ever noticed that certain people just drain the kindness right out of you?

Who, why, how, and when?

JULY 31

Get yourself into the game of life!

Most people just want to make it to retirement. Most people tiptoe through their lives.

Where's the meaning in that?

As Sheryl Sandberg says, lean in.

What does it mean to 'lean in' at the table?

Why or why aren't you leaning in?

AUGUST

AUGUST 1

"Knowing yourself is the

beginning of all wisdom."

~Aristotle~

Do not let a single day pass by without getting something done, however small it might be.

Create an accomplishment list from Birth to now. Notice how much you have accomplished.

How do achievements make you wiser? Describe one that made you wiser.

AUGUST 2

Do not strive to be well known. Strive to be worth knowing.

What are you doing in your life that you are known for?

What is your special niche, and how is it helping the world?

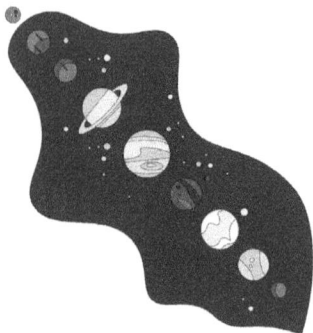

AUGUST 3

It has been my observation that if a team runs effectively for six months without a manager, you should not hire a new manager; you should promote from within!

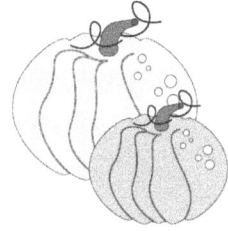

Here are a few mistakes that new managers make:

> They work in a silo.
>
> They make too many changes all at once.
>
> They don't spend time getting to know the individuals on their team.
>
> They become buddies with someone on the team.
>
> They are general and indirect.
>
> They ignore performance concerns.
>
> They show a lack of confidence.
>
> They micro-manage people who don't need it.
>
> They don't share enough knowledge or the right level of it.

What 3 things can you do to promote *cooperation* within a team?

AUGUST 4

Green flags in people.

They celebrate your wins.

They remember small things about you.

They respect your boundaries.

You feel energized after seeing them.

They listen without being defensive.

They make you feel safe.

You don't have to watch what you say.

They do not show two faces.

They support your goals.

AUGUST 5

The Tao Te Ching.

There is a difference between spirituality and religion.

You were born with spirit. You were taught religion.

Describe your spiritual connection with a higher power.

Do you believe in something greater than yourself? Why or why not?

AUGUST 6

An owl is a symbolic bird of wisdom.

The more it sees, the less it takes.

The more it hears, the less it partakes.

What are you partaking in? Why?

What are the positives and negatives of partaking in hot topics?

AUGUST 7

Thoughts come and go; they are like visitors. You don't have to give credence to every thought that comes into your head. Your neurons randomly keep firing and adjusting all day and night long.

You have the power, through free will, to transform those thoughts. Some people transform triggers into glimmers. Glimmers are those moments in your day that bring you peace and happiness. But you have to train your brain to look for the glimmers.

Back brain perception: "Darn. It's raining. I hate driving in the rain. Maybe I'll call in sick."

Frontal lobe perception: "Darn. It's raining. Although I don't like driving in the rain, I can take it slower on the road."

Perspicacity: "The Earth's trees need to be watered."

What is transformation?

How do you transform your head-heart-gut brains to gain *perspicacity*?

AUGUST 8

You can change by changing your vibes. Everything vibes. Peace, love, and understanding vibe much higher than anger, shame, and guilt.

As you raise your vibration, you shift. You no longer resonate with negativity or with those who have a lower frequency than you.

Your world will change. Your experiences will change. It doesn't mean that you are working in isolation, but rather that you will attract people with the same high vibes that you have created for yourself.

You may become a threat to those who are vibrating much lower. They are stuck, and they surely do not understand that they have the power and free will to vibrate higher instead of wishing they were you.

Some people may become offended because that's what people do most of the time. They may be offended by your mere presence.

Stand firm. Hold your high frequency during times of duress.

The universe is for you.

How can you vibe higher?

AUGUST 9

Have you figured out what the signs of a perspicaciously intelligent person are yet?

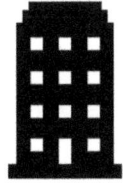

Content Knowledge – you have to know something about something you are passionate about.

Solution-oriented. Not emotion-based.

Logic over feelings.

Critical thinking and accurate memory.

Flexibility, not rigidity.

Reasoning power and sound decision-making.

Empathy, because if you do not have it then it means you are a sociopath and on the DSM scale. Ouch!

Are you perspicaciously intelligent? Why or why not?

AUGUST 10

Human beings communicate through energy. Personality is energy. Before you even utter a word, your frequency relays information into the space that you enter.

Your communication and frequency are transmitted through nonverbal communication.

Some dogs like each other, while others don't.

What type of energy do you emit? Why? How?

AUGUST 11

Fill in the Blanks.

The most descriptive habit is _____.

The greatest loss is _____.

The most satisfying work is _____.

The most upsetting personality trait is _____.

The greatest issue to overcome is _____.

The most powerful means of communication is _____.

The most confident attire is _____.

The most dangerous act is _____.

The most worthless emotion is _____.

The worst weapon is _____.

The greatest joy is _____.

AUGUST 12

Humanism is an approach that believes in Free Will. This philosophy adopts a holistic approach that focuses on a person's needs, potential, self-discovery, and will. It is based on the existential assumption that people are motivated to achieve and self-actualize through capacity, choice, direction, and discipline.

Based on this definition, are you Humanistic? Why or why not?

AUGUST 13

As humans, we have terrible memories.

That's why we must use tools and strategies to help us remember people, places, and things.

Working Memory can hold and manipulate information for cognitive tasks performed in daily life.

Working memory holds information in seven temporary slots.

Working memory can hold only seven items at a time, so it has a small capacity.

Working memory holds and manipulates those pieces of information.

Working memory requires attention, focus, and effort.

AUGUST 14

Your brain will constantly rewire itself to match
the information that you feed your brain.

This rewiring and shifting is Neuroplasticity.

If you complain, gossip, and find excuses, then
it will make it easier for you to find those things to be upset about.

If you search for trouble, you will find it.

If you search for opportunities, you will find them.

This takes self-discipline and practice.

As Dorothy once said in the Wizard of Oz, "You have always had the
power."

What is your dream? Where do you want it to take you? Why?

AUGUST 15

Buy one, get one free!

When you buy into jealousy, your body systems break down. Jealousy does not make any sense because you are losing your mind over other people's goals.

When you buy into anger, you get stomach aches.

When you buy into hate, you get ulcers.

When you buy into stress, you get high blood pressure.

When you buy into burnout, you get mentally imbalanced.

When you buy into distrust, you get communication breakdowns.

When you buy into hate, you can even give yourself cancer.

Laziness kills ambition, while anger kills wisdom. Ambition kills laziness, while anger kills wisdom. Fear kills action, while action kills fear. Jealousy kills growth, while growth kills jealousy. See how this works?

What are you buying? Breakdowns or Breakthroughs? Why or why not?

AUGUST 16

There are a few laws in life.

Which one stands out for you? Why?

Murphy's Law states that the more you fear something, the more it will happen.

Kidlin's Law states that if you can write the problem down with clarity, then the matter is half solved.

Gilbert's Law states that the biggest problem at work is that no one tells you what to do.

Watson's Law states that if you put information and intelligence first, then the money will keep flowing. Many people are smarter than you, not because they are more capable, but because they have more information than you do. Don't lose sight of something powerful: information.

Fakland's Law states that when you do not have to decide, then do not make the decision.

AUGUST 17

Metacognition is the art of "thinking about how you think."

What strategies do you use to include different perspectives?

Why do you think the way you do?

In one Seinfeld episode, George said he was going to do the opposite of what he was thinking because he didn't trust his thinking anymore.

What if you thought the opposite of what you are currently thinking?

There is something called "Strategic Umbrage" (uses by FBI investigator, Chris Voss), which means – everything you do counts. The problem is: you only count the things you think count!

Your manager lacks strategic thinking skills. How can you help them grow as a leader?

AUGUST 18

Faulty Thinking.

Mind-reading: You know what the other person is thinking, so you don't listen to their words.

Jumping to conclusions: You know what's going to happen, so you assume and conclude.

Listening to reply: You don't listen to their words. You're busy thinking about what you're going to say.

Should have. Could have. Would have: Regrets.

All or nothing: It's always or never; there is no in-between.

Unfair comparisons: Comparing your level to someone else.

Labeling: Giving labels to people, places, and things.

Emotional reasoning: Disregarding facts and logic.

Generalizing: Something that applies to all of them.

What faulty thinking are you stuck in? How can you change that?

AUGUST 19

How can you master your mind?

Right now, you are thinking of your head, mind, heart, and gut as separate entities. All twelve body systems work together simultaneously.

You cannot solely work on one organ in your body. All organs are connected through systems, blood, and nutrient transport.

Connect your mind with your heart-brain, and not to worldly chaos. The reason why this identification distorts your metacognition and perception is because it is misaligned.

Turn the mind's circus into something constructive and productive by connecting all three brains.

Can you master your mind? Why or why not?

AUGUST 20

Sadguru is a famous guru from India. He makes the distinction between true love and fake love.

Back brain perception: Love is when you get along all the time.

Frontal lobe perception: Love takes skills and reasoning.

Perspicacity: Love takes acceptance. Love takes discernment.

What is true love to you? What is fake love to you?

AUGUST 21

Back brain perception: I need to find love to have a fulfilling life.

Frontal lobe perception: Maybe I will find true love, and maybe I will not.

Perspicacity: I will find meaning and purpose in life unrelated to true love.

Is it possible to have a fulfilling life without finding true love? Why or why not?

AUGUST 22

The Silent Generation consists of traditionalists and conformists who want stability.

The Boomer Generation is brand loyal, hardworking, and cautious.

Generation X is independent, resourceful, and entrepreneurial.

Generation Y loves quality is tech-loyal and wants to be global citizens.

Generation Z is technical and communal, and values experiences.

The Alpha generation loves everything virtual.

Which Generation do you come from? What are your values?

AUGUST 23

"There is no such thing as Free Will," *exclaimed behaviorist and psychologist B.F. Skinner.*

Do you agree or disagree with him?

Why or why not?

AUGUST 24

Every action creates energy that returns in like kind.

Choosing actions that bring helpfulness and joy generates good energy that returns to you.

You always have the power to make a choice.

The fruits of your labor depend on your choices.

How do you know when it's time to let go of a goal? What goal have you let go of in the past, and why?

AUGUST 25

Everyone has their own distinct purpose in life.

Everyone has their own gift to give to this world.

Embracing your uniqueness attracts wisdom.

Using your gifts to help others creates abundance.

What is the hardest decision you had to make at work?

In personal life?

Why did you have to make it?

What did you learn?

How did you evolve from that experience to gain *perspicacity*?

AUGUST 26

Are you living in the Past, Present, or Future?

Dwelling in the Past brings you guilt and shame.

Obsessing about the Future brings you fear and anxiety.

Staying in the Present brings you sufficient management of work and life.

Your Conscious Mind analyzes, plans, judges, and perceives. It works mainly through Short-term Memory.

Your Sub-Conscious Mind has Long-term Memory, which contains emotions and feelings, habits and patterns, relationship models and addictions, involuntary body functions, developmental stages, creativity and intuition, and spiritual connections. As we move through life's developmental stages, I want to call them "Levels", and even "Levels of Accomplishment". Attention allows you to move towards growth, perspicacity, and wisdom. Those things that do not garner your attention are left unattended and ignored.

AUGUST 27

The Fable of the "Turtle and Hare" is a fable about a race between a rabbit and a turtle. Everyone thought the rabbit would win, but he needed a long rest, and the turtle won the race instead.

Describe a time when you assumed that something would happen, and it did not.

AUGUST 28

What you think becomes your mind.

What you feel becomes your mood.

What you eat becomes your body.

What you say becomes your truth.

What you love becomes your passion.

What you see becomes your perspective.

What you connect becomes your spirit.

What are you thinking, feeling, eating, saying, loving, seeing, and connecting most of the time?

AUGUST 29

Surrender is not about quiet quitting.

Surrender is about giving up the need for control and listening to your wise spirit.

There is a difference between force and flow. When you are forcing things, they don't work out. When you are in flow, miracles happen.

Synchronicities can be energy when you find flow and allow yourself to be guided by your spirit.

Surrender can be a portal to great things.

Is it more important to focus on the journey or destination in life? Why or why not?

AUGUST 30

Life is like the photos that you love to peruse.

You can use the negatives to develop into something greater.

What do you see when you see pictures from the past? The present? Which ones are your favorite? Why?

AUGUST 31

What are 3 freedoms that you enjoy?

Why are they so important to you?

Back brain perception: I want a Big Mac.

Frontal lobe perception: I don't have it often.

Perspicacity: This Big Mac costs five dollars, *and* it costs me my *health*.

———————

Back brain perception: I want to binge-watch this weekend.

Frontal lobe perception: I had a hard week, so I deserve something I enjoy.

Perspicacity: Binge-watching is not free, and it will cost me *time*.

———————

Back brain perception: I love cat videos.

Frontal lobe perception: Watching cat videos puts me in a good mood.

Perspicacity: Social media is not free; it costs me my focus and attention.

SEPTEMBER

SEPTEMBER 1

Metacognition is not easy.

That's why most people judge; judging comes easily.

How do you manage Uncertainty in different environments?

When you are in the sun, it warms, charges, heals, illuminates, nourishes, and produces Vitamin D.

When you are in the moon, it clears, renews, manifests, and enhances intuition.

When you are in the ocean, it cleanses, releases, invigorates, and refreshes.

When you are in the forest, it stabilizes, balances, grounds, and connects.

SEPTEMBER 2

"The child who is not embraced by the village will burn it down to feel its warmth."

~African Proverb~

What does this proverb mean to you and for your life and the society that you live in?

SEPTEMBER 3

Some psychology facts that always get my attention:

Being forgetful is a sign of high intelligence.

Not arguing in a relationship indicates a lack of interest.

People are most honest when they are tired.

People are more likely to tell you the truth after a laugh.

Seven other people in this world look like you do, and you will never meet them.

You become a new person each year because your interests, focus, and desires change with time.

Which one darts out at you, and why?

SEPTEMBER 4

Take ownership of your actions through the realization that nothing is permanent, and that everything is connected to another.

A client said: "I walked away because they were too busy finding faults in me while I was too busy overlooking theirs. They thought that being nice was weak while I was creating psychological safety, empowering others, making team cohesiveness a priority, ensuring teammates felt valued, feeling culturally humble, and responding to constructive feedback."

What is the *perspicacity* here?

SEPTEMBER 5

The story of how long it takes a bamboo tree to grow always fascinates me. For five years, the Bamboo seed stays dormant in the ground. It is in the fifth year that the bamboo tree grows to be a hundred feet tall.

Good things take time.

The day you plant a seed in the ground is not the day you eat the fruit.

What good thing have you waited a long time for? Was it worth the wait? Why or why not?

SEPTEMBER 6

How long is your "I'm offended" list?

Being offended is a form of narcissism mixed with below-average intelligence and a lack of empathy.

If you do nothing else this year, refuse to be offended.

People get addicted to feeling offended because it gives them a sense of importance. Feeling self-righteous and superior always makes the ego feel important.

A big part of adulting (aka maturing) is being able to allow others to express their opinions without getting offended or defensive.

You will continue to bring suffering into your body if you choose to have an emotional reaction to everything that someone says to you.

Your being offended is your responsibility. It is not other people's responsibility to tiptoe around you on eggshells.

A wise person once said that we are living in a time where intelligent people are being silenced so that stupid people will not get offended by their common sense.

Just because you are offended does not mean that you are right!

People who are guilty of mistreating you are offended by everything you say and do.

Tolerance will reach such a level that intelligent people will be banned from thinking so as not to offend the imbeciles. ~Fyodor Dostoevsky~

SEPTEMBER 7

Both fear and faith demand that you believe in something you cannot see. Fear blurts: 'What If,' while faith whispers: 'Even If.'

Do you have unshakable faith?

Do you trust the Spirit within you? Why or why not?

SEPTEMBER 8

No one wants to admit they are flawed. The ego simply will not allow it to happen.

Get real today and think about times when you were insecure, conceited, or dishonest with yourself and others. Admission is just as important as acceptance. Please do not think about these things before you go to bed, though, because you don't want to ruminate right before you go to sleep.

When you are more dishonest, insecure, and unethical you attract more of it. What can you do to become more honest, empathetic, secure, and ethical in your thinking and being?

SEPTEMBER 9

Reflect on an early childhood memory.

Name 2 feelings that come up.

Name 2 emotions that come up.

Name 2 lessons learned.

SEPTEMBER 10

Red flags in us look like this:

Basing our worth on other's approval.

Allowing people to cross boundaries.

Making excuses for other people's behavior.

Not speaking up for fear of conflict.

Self-deprecating.

SEPTEMBER 11

Got Conflict? Ask yourself:

Have I communicated what I'm feeling?

Have I used "I" statements?

Am I bringing in past issues and mixing them in with this one? Are they doing the same?

Am I working with or against this person?

Am I trying to control and persuade this person, or am I actively listening to them?

Am I distracting this person by using faulty thinking?

Is this argument really about something deeper in our relationship?

Am I listening to their feelings and values?

What kind of fighter are you?

What are some prevention and intervention strategies you can use to build peace?

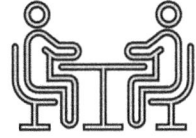

SEPTEMBER 12

Describe the relationships you had with your family.

How do you feel those relationships have shaped your personality, your vocation, and your interests?

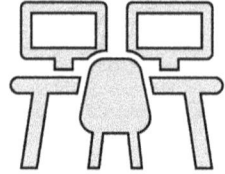

SEPTEMBER 13

If you could relive any day from the past, which one would it be and why?

SEPTEMBER 14

"Write books only if you are going to say in them the things you would never dare confide to anyone."
~Emil Cioran~

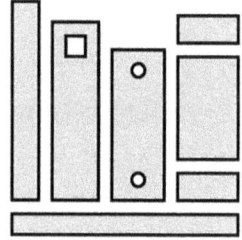

Name 5 of your favorite books.

Write them down and state why they are your favorite ones.

SEPTEMBER 15

Name 5 of your favorite movies.

Why are they your favorites?

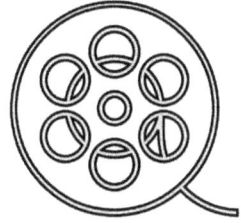

SEPTEMBER 16

Describe a defining moment or 'Aha' moment in your life.

What makes it feel so significant?

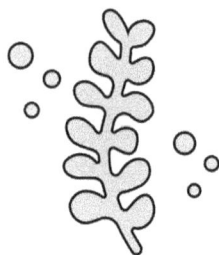

SEPTEMBER 17

Name a situation where you have done each
of the following:

Gave people grace.

Gave people more than they asked for.

Gave good eye contact while apologizing.

Didn't judge anyone.

Wasn't a sore loser.

Open to receiving constructive criticism.

SEPTEMBER 18

There is an old saying that tells us that if animals and babies like you then you are A-okay.

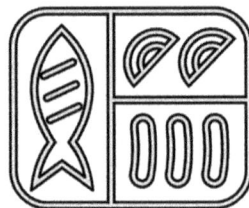

Do animals feel safe with you?

Do people stare at you in public?

Do random strangers love talking to you and telling you stories?

Does the energy of the room shift when you walk in?

Do you irritate toxic people?

Do you have a high sense of empathy?

Do you feel grateful most of the time?

Do you attract positive people? If so, your dopamine will increase.

Do you steer clear of drama? If not, your stress hormones (cortisol & adrenaline will increase inside your sympathetic nervous system).

Perspicacity: Toxic people never want to discuss the cruel things they say or think about you. All they want to do is talk about your reactions, how crazy you are, or how you need help. They completely deflect their own behavior and claim that you are unstable and have no right to be hurt by what they say and do to you.

SEPTEMBER 19

Manners are of utmost importance.

Which ones do you forget, and why?

Say please and thank you. They are still the magic words.

Do not interrupt people when they are talking.

If someone says hello, then say it back.

Ditch political correctness here and open doors for men and women.

Close your mouth when you are eating.

Sneeze into your elbow.

Do not complain when someone is helping you.

Wash your hands before each meal.

Pick up your trash and throw it in the garbage bin, not out the car window.

Push your chair in and take your plate to the sink.

If you bump into someone, say excuse me.

Write thank-you notes.

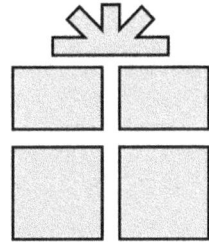

SEPTEMBER 20

What makes someone a hero?

SEPTEMBER 21

Marriage is not the end of the search for love.
It's the end of the search for a person to love.
The search for ways to love that
person has just begun.
~Frank Sinatra~

Finish this sentence.

A great partner is like having...

SEPTEMBER 22

The essence of great leadership is empathy, not authority. When you sit with warriors, the conversation and mindset feels different.

I invite you to cultivate certain skills to understand self-leading: emotional regulation, self-discipline, forgiveness, mindfulness, and consistency.

People at work and in your personal life will bring out your triggers, wounds, fears, and insecurities.

When do you feel this way at work? In personal life?

What can be learned, and what can be done?

SEPTEMBER 23

One of my favorite books is "Woman's Inhumanity to Woman" by Phyllis Chesler because she addresses the conditioning of women. She provides studies, evidence, and solutions for female aggression toward one another.

She delves into lifespan development, anthropology, and literature to state that competition between women has overtaken their natural tendency towards friendships.

Have you noticed competition, envy, mistrust, and dislike among women?

What can be done to rectify this conditioning?

What are some expectations that you need to let go of? Why?

SEPTEMBER 24

Before sharing something with someone, say these things.

Do you have the emotional bandwidth to listen to me vent about something?

Is this a good time to talk about how I'm feeling?

Do you have a few minutes for me? I want to process a situation with you.

Do you have the mental space to listen to something?

I've had a stressful day, and I need to vent. Are you in a strong emotional space to listen to me?

I'm having a bad day, but you are, too, so are you available to talk for a while?

Dr. Hans Selye connected his patients' ailments with work stress. What is happening at your job that is causing you to stress out? How can you manage that stress? What coping strategies are you using?

SEPTEMBER 25

What is the difference between a relationship and a partnership?

SEPTEMBER 26

Here are some elements of a relationship:

Respect isn't always present. Needs are often unmet. What needs have you been trying to meet since childhood? Uneven power dynamics. Lack of emotional safety. Most days are on autopilot.

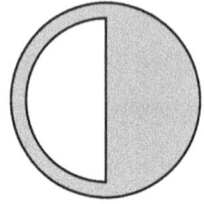

Here are the elements of a partnership:

Mutual respect. Anticipation of needs. Difficult conversations are not so difficult. Actions align with words. Each takes responsibility for mistakes and grows. Prioritizes shared goals. You are there because you want to be there.

How do you create a safe environment for people at work and home?

Here is some wisdom: Process information without getting defensive. Don't assume the worst and listen to understand without emotions clouding your ears.

SEPTEMBER 27

I would rather spend my life with someone kind and not educated rather than intelligent and unkind.

True or false? Why?

SEPTEMBER 28

Hormones are different from Neurotransmitters. Hormones come from the Endocrine System, while Neurotransmitters come from the Nervous System. Hormones spill into the bloodstream and last longer than neurotransmitters.

There are famous Neurotransmitters:

Endorphins give you good feelings, euphoria, and a sense of well-being.

Serotonin gives you emotional stability, self-confidence, pain tolerance, and quality of sleep.

There are famous Hormones:

Adrenaline gives you a rush and the ability to flight or fight.

Oxytocin gives you a sense of belonging when touched or loved.

Dopamine gives you good feelings, comfort, and alertness.

Describe some situations where you have felt these Hormones and Neurotransmitters working.

SEPTEMBER 29

Would you rather hire someone who has life skills or job skills?

Why or why not?

SEPTEMBER 30

This month went by quickly. The stores have Halloween and Thanksgiving décor, and some even have Christmas decorations already.

This year brought you a new beginning, just as the start of each year. Each new year, you vow to discard destructive old habits for healthy new ones.

Today, refrain from improving others but yourself. How?

Your power move today will be to arrive ten minutes early. Build rapport. Compliment another. Mirror their positive energy. Manage delays with grace. Scan the room with confidence without dominance. Match the pace of another. Stay calm during chaos and crises.

"I appreciate you letting me know" is a great phrase to keep in your back pocket.

OCTOBER

OCTOBER 1

Question everything your mind thinks.

Don't accept your thinking at face value.

Ask your brain if this is true? Where's the evidence?

Analyze your thoughts from a different perspective.

Locate the Bias.

Use logic and reasoning rather than emotions and feelings.

Ask yourself "Who, why, when, where, and how" questions, before you believe everything your mind tells you to be the absolute truth.

There is a 51% divorce rate in the Western Hemisphere. Is this stat high or low, in your estimation? Why?

OCTOBER 2

Did you know that part of learning also includes how to unlearn?

Yes, the brain's function is to learn; but it can also unlearn and relearn things.

How about a few things to unlearn? Like trying to change people or yelling to get your way or trying to win an argument or comparing yourself to others or assuming the worst?

What are the 3 things you love most about your workplace?

OCTOBER 3

Mahatma Gandhi's philosophy was "Passive Resistance Non-violence." MLK adopted this philosophy for his Civil Rights Movement for Black people.

Create a peacebuilding philosophy.

OCTOBER 4

What are 3 things that you love about your personal life?

Why did you choose these?

OCTOBER 5

Fyodor Dostoevdky said:

"To live without hope is to cease to live."

Name 3 things that give you Hope for the future. Why did you choose these things?

OCTOBER 6

The leaves are changing, the apples are crunchy, and the pumpkin spice lattes are hot.

What do you love about the four seasons of the year? What is your favorite season, and why? Which season makes you most productive? Why?

OCTOBER 7

Being glued to your phone or computer is called a process addiction.

What process addiction do you have?

How can you rectify it?

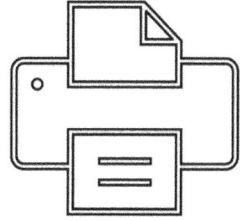

OCTOBER 8

You will continue to bring suffering into your body if you continue to take things personally. Learn to separate business and personal. Decisions must be made quickly, and not everything is about you.

Shift your perspective. Get your head on straight.

Practice self-compassion. Practice to get thick skin.

Learn how you communicate and be transparent. Be mindful.

Have positive self-talk. Say positive affirmations.

Check your locus of control.

Focus on the things you can control and allow your higher power to take control of the rest.

Cultivate a good sense of humor without being cynical or sarcastic.

What else?

OCTOBER 9

Anam Cara: a person with whom you can share your deepest thoughts, feelings, and dreams; a soul friend.

Who is your best friend?

Why are they your best friend?

What qualities do they have?

How do you know you can trust and love them?

OCTOBER 10

The Chinese culture has poetic, philosophical, and practical wisdom. They gave this world Lao Tzu, Sun Tzu, and Confucious. They gave us the Tao Te Ching, which is filled with wisdom.

Here is an example of a Chinese proverb: *"When the winds of change blow, some people build walls while others build windmills"*.

When change happens, some people resist it by building walls, but others adapt and build windmills. There is a difference between the people who fear change and those who use it as an opportunity to build something new.

> *"The soul has no secret that the behavior does not reveal."*
> ~Lao Tzu~

What does Lao Tzu mean?

OCTOBER 11

What you desire is being manifested through the law of attraction.

What you believe, you attract.

What you think, you attract.

To attract better, you need to become better.

Whatever is on your mind, will appear.

To become perspicacious, you need to have a code that looks for wisdom.

What is your "code"?

How do you find wisdom? How do you use wisdom?

OCTOBER 12

Write a scene that takes place during a conflict.

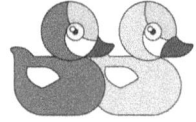

OCTOBER 13

When you meet someone from another culture, say this: What is it about your culture that you would like me to know?

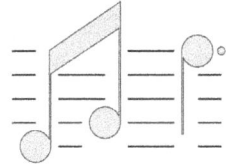

This is called "Cultural Humility."

How do you include people to give them a sense of belonging?

OCTOBER 14

Learn to self-lead before accepting a leadership role. Self-leading includes positive and *responsible* self-talk:

I wonder....

Why do you think of....

What does this remind you of?

What did I see?

What did I hear?

What do I already know?

What more do I need to know?

Be a wise leader!

What other questions can you add to your self-talk?

OCTOBER 15

Where do you see yourself in 5 years' time?

My answer: I am going to mentor more. I am going to increase my leadership responsibilities. I am going to solve new challenges. I am going to provide understanding through active listening in order to build peaceful workplaces, families, communities, organizations, and large audiences everywhere in the world. I am going to be a wise leader."

Now write <u>your</u> answer here.

OCTOBER 16

Kurt Vonnegut said:

"We are what we pretend to be, so we must be careful what we pretend to be."

I am pretending about..........

OCTOBER 17

Which sentence makes you stronger?

Everyone leaves, so I must learn to survive alone.

I value my experiences over possessions and cherish memories.

I seek knowledge and wisdom over all else.

I love time management and spend time wisely on what truly matters.

I show inner strength through compassion.

I find solace when I am alone.

I am grateful for my job and people.

I am content and not obsessing over or chasing happiness.

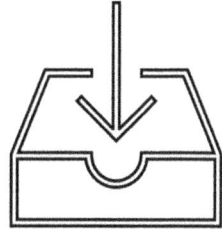

OCTOBER 18

I saw this on Pinterest and thought it was good.

Talk to a mother lovingly.

Talk to a father respectfully.

Talking to a wife truthfully.

Talk to a brother heartfully.

Talk to a sister affectionately.

Talk to kids enthusiastically.

Talk to relatives empathetically.

Talk to friends joyfully.

Talk to officials politely.

Talk to Internal (colleagues) and External (strangers) customers politely.

How do you talk to people?

Do you hold a polite tone with colleagues as well as for strangers and clients? Why or why not?

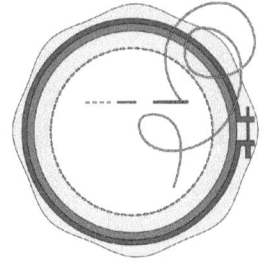

OCTOBER 19

Things you do not learn in school:

How to inspect thinking through metacognition and strategic umbrage.

How to negotiate.

How to face failure.

How to invest money.

How to find your passion.

How to be an entrepreneur.

How to start a business.

How to read paychecks and bank statements.

How to do taxes.

How to invest money.

How to study.

How to manage time.

Add 3 more things to this list. Why do you think that schools do not teach these things? What can you do about it?

OCTOBER 20

A fact is information minus emotion.

An opinion is information plus experience.

Ignorance is an opinion lacking information.

Idiocy is an opinion that ignores facts.

Foolishness is the Dunning-Kreuger Effect when someone thinks they know everything but know nothing, and they don't realize that they know nothing.

What do you do if you have someone foolish on your team?

OCTOBER 21

Two contradictory things can coexist. Agree or disagree, and why?

I'm making progress and am struggling.

I don't have to shoot for perfection, but I do want to perfect a certain skill.

I'm processing my trauma, but I still get triggered.

I make decisions, but there are times when I am undecided.

I have days that make me feel great, and then there are others that get me down.

I get things done, but sometimes I procrastinate.

OCTOBER 22

Agree or disagree? Why or why not?

My brain, without goals, will always focus on what's wrong.

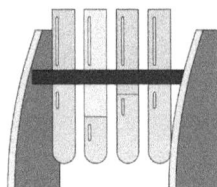

My brain, without goals, will ruminate over situations and people.

My brain, without goals, will repeat past mistakes.

My brain without goals will create fear.

My brain without goals will create anxiety.

My brain without goals will create worry.

My brain without goals will create confusion.

OCTOBER 23

Do you work with toxic people?

They make everything into an issue.

They are dramatic.

They are unsupportive. They are not helpful.

They are out for themselves. They have a big ego.

They never admit their mistakes. They always blame others.

They lie, cheat, and steal. They gossip and make up rumors.

They are ungrateful attention seekers, argumentative, and dominators. They are unproductive and irresponsible. They are opinionated spectators.

Know that the true luxuries in life are time, health, peace, travel, rest, good food, good-natured people, and calm. Not guilt or shame, no doubt or blame.

How would you help a colleague overcome self-doubt through a coaching type conversation through with constructive feedback and positive reinforcement?

OCTOBER 24

Neuro-dots that connect and ignite neuro-sparks (my term) in the brain help you get closer to **_perspicacity_**. The brain responds positively to wisdom. Neurons fire and you can feel the sparkles through your heart-brain neurons.

How can you move quicker from the back brain perception to the frontal lobe perception and to perspicacity?

Hint: Metacognition and strategic umbrage.

OCTOBER 25

Accountability feels like an attack when you're not open to acknowledging how your behavior affects others.

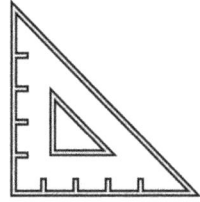

Emails often feel like an attack because the non-verbal's are not there so there is much left to the interpretation of the reader at the time they are reading the email. The back brain is the default setting! Anything you read or hear will go to the back brain first. It is your Free Will, awareness, and intention that can bring your thoughts away from feelings and into the rational front brain.

What is the **perspicacity** here?

OCTOBER 26

Never make the mistake of assuming that
the peacebuilder is unskilled at war.

What does this mean to you?

Have you ever been blindsided? What happened?

OCTOBER 27

People behave differently at work - loud, quiet, serene, bombastic, funny, and grumpy, and they even avoid, compete, confront, accommodate, or compromise.

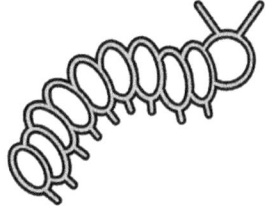

Describe situations where you were all of these.

OCTOBER 28

There are many ways that you can express respect and love for others. Here is some relationship wisdom for you:

1. Texting is only for quickie things like groceries, flirting, or location. Do not use texting for fighting, arguing, or serious discussions.
2. Don't discuss your wife's or husband's shortcomings with your family, coworkers, or boss.
3. Nothing is gained when two people are yelling. When both are calm, then you can have a constructive dialogue for understanding.
4. A solution is something that is proper when both people agree to it, and not just one.

How will you learn how to fight with civility?

OCTOBER 29

Is a plan a strategy, or are they different?

A Strategy is a logical theory that is a choice, whereas a Plan is a process with action steps.

How do you build trust, safety, and respect at work? At home?

OCTOBER 30

People can steal material things, but they can never take away your knowledge.

What is something you know that no one else knows?

OCTOBER 31

Did you know that you pass your death day each passing year?

Why do we continue frivolously if we are not guaranteed a future?

NOVEMBER

NOVEMBER 1

Your real competition is the following items, and these take **perspicacity** to change.

The knowledge you neglect to learn. Lack of discipline.

Distractions. Habits. Doubts.

Ego. Procrastination. Narrow mindedness.

Closed mindset. Difficult.

Wisdom is poetic, philosophical, and practical.

How do you compete against yourself? Until you make the unconscious conscious, you will continue to live a life that you believe is through fate.

NOVEMBER 2

The more you research, the crazier you sound to ignorant folks.

There are two types of people: those that think through lack, and those who think abundantly.

If they lack accountability, they will shift the blame to you.

If they lack communication skills, they will say you are arguing.

If they lack emotional intelligence, they will criticize you.

If they lack honesty, they will distort information.

If they lack empathy, run the other way.

Cmdr. Rorke Denver (a Navy SEAL) has the best piece of advice: "Calm is contagious."

The thing that I have learned about living in military housing with SEALs is that they have trained themselves to have the ability to be comfortable in chaos and this is their competitive advantage other others!

What fascinates you most about humans, their nature, and their behavior?

NOVEMBER 3

In your opinion, which is more important?

Genetics or environment? Why?

NOVEMBER 4

What are the most common misconceptions about human behavior? Your behavior?

If you came with a small label (like a T-shirt has on the neck) what would it say?

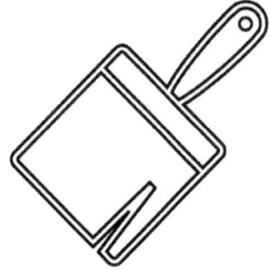

"I promise if you keep searching for everything beautiful in this world, you will eventually become it."

~Tyler Kent White~

NOVEMBER 5

What are your top 3 Needs?

What are your top 3 Wants?

What is the difference between your Needs and Wants?

NOVEMBER 6

Talk about a time that you were manipulated.

How did it feel, and what did you learn from that experience?

Afraid to disagree.

Felt anxious and fearful.

Felt confused and perplexed.

Felt like you were going crazy.

They said they loved you but then said and did horrible things to you.

They twisted, minimized, and invalidated everything you said.

They punished you.

They insulted you.

They made fun of you and told you it was a joke.

They said you were too sensitive.

They said you always take things the wrong way.

NOVEMBER 7

Just imagine being bitten by a poisonous spider, and instead of trying to help yourself heal and recover, you go after the spider to find out the reason it bit you, and then you try to prove to it that you did not deserve to be bitten.

Does this make any sense to you? Why or why not?

In some cultures, the spider is the symbol of patience because she waits and waits.

Look at life through the triad of the head-heart-gut brains. Remember these perspicacious things:

1. Feel the feelings, then try again.
2. Each day is a brand-new day and another chance to be wise.
3. Cry or throw up but never quit your dream.
4. Empathize, love, get burned, then empathize and love again.

NOVEMBER 8

Life advice:

Not everyone will like you.

Everyone gossips. They will gossip about you.

Failure does not have anything to do with your potential.

You cannot change your past.

You cannot change others; you can only change yourself.

You cannot control others; you can only control yourself.

If you are a slug, you cannot gargle with salt and water! (Common sense).

Happiness comes from within.

Stress arrives when there is a breach of something you value.

Failing does not undermine your value.

Not everything will go your way, and that's okay.

You will not have closure for everything in life.

You cannot manipulate every detail of life.

The sooner you learn how to pivot from the irrational back brain perception, the closer you will be to wisdom.

Your **perspicacity**?

NOVEMBER 9

Quiet Quitting.

Go to work late in the morning.

Leave work early.

Come back from lunch late.

Do as little as possible.

Talk to colleagues and spend less time at your desk.

Put in the least amount of effort.

Work slowly.

Don't meet deadlines.

Use templates.

Keep your resume and references updated.

Take all your vacation and sick days.

Have you done any of these things? Where, when, and why? What did you learn?

NOVEMBER 10

Do you have Stinkin' Thinkin'?

"It's amazing how many people are ashamed of their bodies but how few of their minds."

~Andrzej Saramonowicz~

If people make a mistake, they apologize (at least most do), and they continue living their days. They rarely analyze what happened and what they would do differently the next time.

What you eat, you become. What you think, you become. Just as you have to eat healthy and exercise, the same goes for the mind too. Your thoughts become actions that become habits (Lao Tzu).

What needs to improve in your mind?

NOVEMBER 11

Perfect your Life Skills. Which ones do you need to improve? Why?

Selling.

Writing

Speaking.

Investing.

Marketing.

Budgeting.

Networking.

Negotiating.

Self-control. This is an important one! Self-control is brave. You have to get to a point where your emotions do not sweep you away due to the actions of someone else. Do not allow others to control you. Do not allow your feelings and emotions to override your logic, reasoning, and IQ.

Decision-making.

Taking responsibility.

Problem-solving.

Time-management.

Financial independence.

Effective Communication.

NOVEMBER 12

Have you ever walked away from someone or something?

When should you walk away?

When:

They don't allow you to speak your truth.

They don't allow you to express your feelings.

They dismiss what you say.

They minimize or invalidate you.

They are committed to misunderstanding you.

Why make fun of you?

They gaslight or stonewall.

They withhold information.

They withdraw.

They play the victim.

They are the jealous type.

They do not share your joy.

Did you know that 90% of conflicts occur due to the tone of voice and not the words?

NOVEMBER 13

When people go through traumatic experiences, as in childhood, they start picturing the worst outcomes to protect themselves from future blindsides. They may speak negatively all the time. This is a defense mechanism that allows them to be prepared for the next time they are blindsided or traumatized. They fear being caught unaware of their vulnerability.

Are you doing this? Do you know someone who does this?

NOVEMBER 14

You struggle to change because the old behavior still meets some needs.

Why do you resist change?

Why are you afraid of change?

> *"The measure of intelligence is the ability to change."*
> ~Albert Einstein~

NOVEMBER 15

If you want more peace in your life, then do these things:

Stop arguing with people.

Stop wasting energy on futile relationships.

Stop trying to fix people.

Stop pretending to be happy.

Stop overthinking.

Stop overlooking your blessings.

Stop trying to change others.

Which ones are you doing? Why?

NOVEMBER 16

Your brain can betray you during a dysfunctional relationship.

The on-and-off cycle of attention followed by neglect or kindness followed by harm creates a trauma bond.

The brain oscillates between releasing oxytocin and cortisol. The instability of these chemicals breeds disease inside the brain, heart, and gut, making you feel fearful and anxious via the amygdala.

Brain chemistry plays a vast role in physical and psychological needs. Safety becomes attainable only after your brain is convinced that you are content and in your parasympathetic nervous system.

How aware are you? What can you do to become more aware?

NOVEMBER 17

"When the character of a man is not clear
to you, just look at his friends."
　　　　~Japanese Proverb~

Be known by the company you keep. Who
are your friends? What jobs do they have? How do they influence you?
What are their values?

NOVEMBER 18

Learn to:

Identify possibilities.

Approach issues as puzzles that must be solved.

Turn a problem into a hypothesis or problem statement to brainstorm solutions.

Test out your hypotheses.

Do more:

Observing.

Consulting.

Communicating.

Motivating.

Inspiring.

Empowering.

Gain more:

Open-mindedness.

Metacognition.

Self-discipline.

NOVEMBER 19

Boost your confidence by:

Meditating. The *perspicacity*: Your brain needs solitude. It was Picasso that said, "without great solitude, there is no serious work."

Mentoring. The *perspicacity*: mentor teams!

Write down your successes, however small. The *perspicacity*: you will see how much you have accomplished in life.

Taking risks. The *perspicacity*: Not taking a risk is taking the most significant risk of all.

Not comparing yourself to others. *Perspicacity*: and others to others!

Dressing up. The *perspicacity*: Clothes make the man and the woman. Don't wait for a special occasion. Just wear it!

Embracing feedback. The *perspicacity*: When it's constructive, it can lead you to great heights.

Saving your money. The *perspicacity*: know your spending habits.

Decluttering your work desk and home. The *perspicacity*: all those items hold energy that affects you.

Creating a Life Code to live by. The *perspicacity*: Create a platinum rule that you never break.

Use reading as a coping strategy to learn, unlearn, and relearn. Take from diverse perspectives and readings by great authors. Read the Tao Te Ching, Rig Vedas and Bhagavad Gita, Upanishads, Mahabharata and Ramyana, the Torah, the Bible, and more!

NOVEMBER 20

If you are an adult, then you are expected to act maturely. In order to act mature, you must also think maturely.

If you don't like someone, don't recruit others to join your cause.

Write about someone you dislike. What qualities do they have? How can you help them? How can you learn to communicate with them?

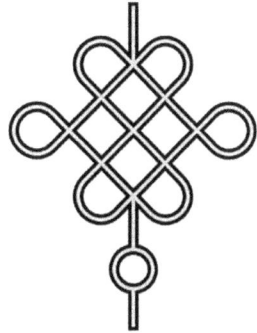

NOVEMBER 21

It's not your job to:

Fix people.

Save people.

Change people.

Chase people.

Make people happy.

Prove people wrong.

Control people.

Control someone's perception of you.

Agree with the room.

Help somebody who did not ask for it.

Try to convince people of what they cannot see.

Try to convince people of what they need.

Why do you try to convince people and do these things?

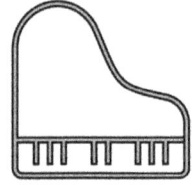

NOVEMBER 22

What 3 Values are nonnegotiable to you, and why?

What Values do you emphasize when decision-making?

Do your Values propel you toward wisdom, or do they keep you stuck in habits and patterns?

Do your Values lead you to integrity or lead you to shame?

Perspicacity You are stuck because you are committed to certain patterns of behavior because they have worked for you in the past. Those behaviors do not work all of the time though, and sometimes they are harmful rather than helpful. The reason why you cannot move forward is because you keep using the same behaviors and habits. It is you that must change, adapt, and evolve to get a different outcome.

NOVEMBER 23

Ways you can build trust:

Share information, both good and bad.

Aim for a win-win, not win-lose. Win-win decision-making is a collaborative and engagement approach that explores options for locating mutually beneficial outcomes. This ensures that both people feel they have gained something.

Show up on time. Actually, when you show up on time, you are late.

Be consistent. Don't be erratic in your mood.

Be collaborative. More importantly, be cooperative.

Allow others to help or take initiative. You don't have to be a know-it-all (even if you do know it all).

Give credit freely and publicly. Everyone has an ego that loves being stroked once in a while.

Find a common cause, not a common enemy. The common cause comes from the rational frontal lobe perception, while the common enemy comes from the irrational back brain perception that loves drama.

NOVEMBER 24

It was Voltaire that said: "Everyman is a creature of the age in which he lives, and few are able to raise themselves above the ideas of the time".

What does your emotional, back brain think about this?

What does your wise mind think about this?

NOVEMBER 25

What is the biggest challenge you have faced this year?

Did someone or something kick you to the curb?

Did you deserve it?

Why or why not?

NOVEMBER 26

Which one of these quotes resonates with you?

1. *It's no use going back to yesterday, because I was a different person then. ~Lewis Carroll~*
    He's telling us that personality is fluid and change is constant.

2. *Man is the only creature who refuses to be who he is. ~Albert Camus~*
    In other words, every creature is their authentic self, except for Homo Sapiens (us).

3. *Without deviation, progress is not possible. ~Frank Zappa~*
    We cannot think the same as we did when we got a problem.

4. *When what you hear and what you see do not match, trust your eyes. ~Dale Renton~*
    Observation is empirical.

5. *Nothing is good. Nothing is bad. It is thinking that makes it so. ~William Shakespeare~*
    We judge too much.

6. *Wise men speak because they have something to say. Fools, because they have to say something. ~Plato~*
    Curb your impulses.

7. *Life is simple, but man insists on making it complex. ~Confucius~*
    Concise thoughts, concise explanations, concise reports, concise presentations.

NOVEMBER 27

All hatred is self-hatred.

Everything you experience is a self-reflection of who you are because it is you who is perceiving and interpreting those things.

Describe 10 things you are grateful for and why you are grateful for them.

NOVEMBER 28

What is the hardest thing about family gatherings?

How can you learn to appreciate family more?

Name a family member for whom you are grateful.

Name a place you are thankful for.

Name a food you are thankful for.

Name a gift you are thankful for.

NOVEMBER 29

By now, you should be self-leading through wisdom and discernment.

Self-leading is about taking charge and doing the good work towards *perspicacity*.

Leading others is not about being in charge. Leading others is about looking after them and helping them meet their goals and dreams.

How well are you self-leading?

How well are you leading others?

NOVEMBER 30

Make a list of 4 things you can delegate.

Who will you delegate these 4 things to? Why?

Your senior executive lacks delegation skills. How can you effectively provide constructive feedback?

DECEMBER

DECEMBER 1

The Biology of You is 75% food choices and 25% movement.

The Psychology of you is 75% purpose and 25% meaning.

The Social of You is 75% listening and 25% speaking.

The Cultural of You is 75% understanding and 25% reading.

The Spiritual of You is 75% giving and 25% receiving.

Eleven months flew by. What three things have you learned about yourself this year?

What is holding you back from happiness?

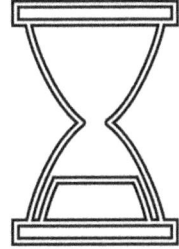

DECEMBER 2

One of my values is to work hard. My immigrant father used to say: Choose your hard because everything is hard. Marriage is hard and so is staying single. Being fit is hard, but so is obesity. Saving money is hard, but so is debt. You must choose your hard!

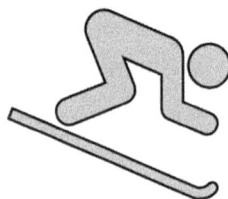

Circle your values. Why did you choose those?

Kindness, Respect, Integrity, Perseverance, Acceptance, Gratitude, Focus, Curiosity, Responsibility, Honesty, Compromise, Interculturalism, Truth, Loyalty, Trust, Open-mindedness, Faith, Hard work, Courage, Optimism.

Spirituality, Empathy, Sense of community, Justice, Patience, Confidence, Humility, Friendship, Fairness, Non-judgment. Adaptation, Change, Sustainability, Unity, Serenity, Harmony.

Being a leader is also hard, because you have to have the skill of being a good follower of instructions, mission, and vision. Recall the Serenity Prayer that make a plea to have the "wisdom to know the difference." The title of this book!! (smiling!).

DECEMBER 3

These are things I have learned as a career practitioner, mediator, and military wife.

There is tremendous grieving for the past.

Healing does not have a time clock.

Connection is vital to existence.

People are always evolving for the better and the worse.

At the end of the day, people just want to be seen and heard.

Baby steps lead to growth.

Certain things should have never happened to you.

We see things by who we are, not by how they really are.

No one sees things the same way.

No one has all the answers to the questions in life.

Empathy is magical.

DECEMBER 4

You have attended master classes. How do you master yourself?

Anything that annoys you is teaching you something about yourself. You need to cultivate patience.

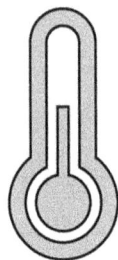

Anyone who abandons you is teaching you how to be independent. Trust yourself.

Anything or anyone that angers you is teaching you about compassion. Get it under control, or else.

Anything you hate is teaching you about love. Give grace.

Anything that makes you afraid is teaching you about courage. Stand tall.

Anything you cannot control is teaching you how to let go of certain things. Focus on what you can get done and leave the rest to the universe.

Anything that stresses you out is teaching you about priorities. Learn to make wise choices. Not everything is about you. Move from ego-centric to wise-centric.

DECEMBER 5

A good friend is someone who...

DECEMBER 6

Describe an instance where something can be true for you but not for someone else.

Write a story about someone that is displaying mental illness behaviors, without mentioning the illness.

DECEMBER 7

If you could change 3 rules at work, what would they be and why?

DECEMBER 8

In-person, remote, or hybrid work?

Why?

DECEMBER 9

Authoritative leadership or Intercultural Leadership?

Why or why not?

DECEMBER 10

Your scientific name comes from the classification system by Dr. Carl Linnaeus. You have a Genus and a Species name. It is "Homo Sapien." You are termed that, in science, because you have a wonderful prefrontal cortex (also known as the Frontal lobe perception). One of the greatest days in your life is going to be when you realize that the world's gurus understood that to change their lives, they had to change their mindsets.

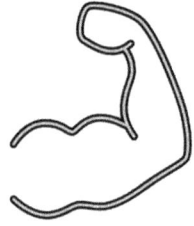

Lao Tzu said: What you believe, you shall become.

Our thoughts and language give us a complex internal world.

A new mindset and a new awareness can create endless possibilities for you. The way you think, adapt, and evolve are the elements and solutions to your fears.

Perspicacity: When you consciously become aware and accept that the issues in your life open doors for you to adopt a better perspective, and then suffering will leave your body, mind, and Spirit. You will flourish and thrive in well-being, purpose, and meaning.

How do your thoughts create your reality?

DECEMBER 11

Being Human is to learn. The brain learns.

Learning **how** to think is critical in formulating a positive mindset, and from that, we can learn how to accept each other, become courageous, and achieve our potential.

What does it mean to be Brave?

Where do you have to be Brave? Why?

DECEMBER 12

Twelve things you need to know to understand who you are.

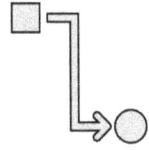

Values are the principles that guide you.

Feelings that describe your emotions.

Inspection of the feelings that you are trying to suppress.

Ambitions are the goals and experiences you want to achieve.

Habits are part of the routine you carry out daily.

Patterns are the consistent ways you think, feel, and act.

Reactions are the way you blurt out things you shouldn't.

Responses are the way you answer through thought and consideration.

Impact is the way you influence others.

Fittest as in the environmental match to your personality.

Difficulties, such as in the hard times, cause pain and suffering.

Perseverance as in the times when you do not give up on yourself.

Spirituality is the time you turn inwards to your inside spirit.

DECEMBER 13

Talk about 3 habits that have become subconscious behaviors that are keeping you from having the life you desire. Habits become routine, and routines create moods.

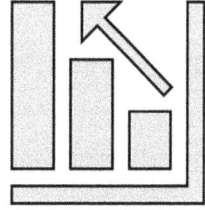

What you have changed this year, and why?

DECEMBER 14

Your back brain perception always wants more and more and more. When is it enough to make you happy?

What are 3 things worth celebrating this month?

DECEMBER 15

Has someone that you once knew, loved, or respected become a stranger? Has someone used cognitive distortions or faulty thinking to burn the bridge?

Uncomfortable feelings indicate that you are on the right path. The uncomfortableness means that you want to do something about it.

What do you want for Christmas this year? Why?

DECEMBER 16

What is something that you wish to be awarded for?

DECEMBER 17

I have a condition where my vocal cords do not close, and that makes my voice wiggle a bit. Some people ask me about it while others do not.

Before you assume, why not just ask?

What is it that you want to ask someone?

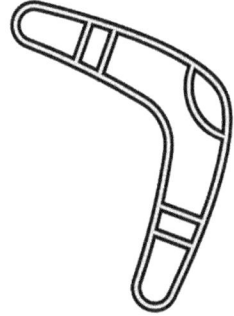

DECEMBER 18

Be open to learn, unlearn, and relearn.

If someone gets the promotion that you wanted, be happy for them.

Your turn is coming. Something better is coming. Always trust the universe. When things don't go your way, they are still going your way!

Talk about a time when you didn't get something you wanted, and then a few months or years later, you learned that it was a good thing that you didn't get it.

DECEMBER 19

Are you sad or happy that this year is ending?

Why?

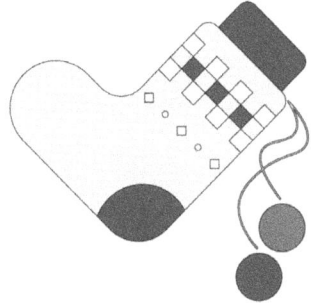

DECEMBER 20

The word Ikigai means "a reason to live."

It comes from a combination of two Japanese words and is a convergence of 4 core elements:

1. What you love. Besides yourself.
2. What the world needs. This world needs wise people with big hearts.
3. What you are good at. Only you know this truth.
4. What you can get paid for. Only you know what you want out of life.

The word Ikigai is viewed as a source of value because it makes one's life worthwhile.

Using the principles of Ikigai, how can you become more joyful?

DECEMBER 21

Create a 5-step plan that will help you to become a better version of yourself in the workplace. And in your personal life.

Hint: Take a close look at the things that you label as unimportant.

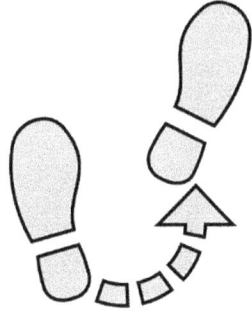

DECEMBER 22

There are things you can change. There are things you cannot change.

How can you tell which is which?

How do you come closer to acceptance?

DECEMBER 23

What is the most courageous thing you've ever done in your life?

How did it make you feel?

How did this lend to gaining more wisdom?

DECEMBER 24

What are your gifts?

What gift are you giving to this world?

DECEMBER 25

Discuss your favorite tradition and why you want to continue it.

DECEMBER 26

Today is the day that people return gifts that don't fit them.

What is one thing, psychologically speaking, that doesn't fit you just right? How can it be transformed?

DECEMBER 27

"There are two things you get each
and every day as you wake up.
A Chance. A Choice."
~J. Prince~

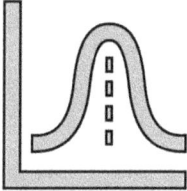

What is one thing you should know how to do by now, but do not?

DECEMBER 28

The most important thing you learn is how to consider the future cost of the decisions you make today.

Talk about 3 things that made you wiser this year.

DECEMBER 29

Talk about something you did not find time to do this year.

DECEMBER 30

What is something you regret doing this year?

What is something you regret <u>not</u> doing this year?

The most important thing you learn is how to consider the future cost of the decisions you make today.

Talk about 3 things that made you wiser this year. What are the things you learned, unlearned, and relearned? How have you become wiser this year?

DECEMBER 31

One of my favorite quotes is from Dr. Robert Schuller. "What would you attempt to do if you knew you could not fail?"

What is something you are looking forward to attempting in the new year?

How have you raised your wisdom and perspicacious intelligence this year?

Write down a new hobby that you will try in the new year.

Pearls of Wisdom To Know The Difference

You have everything you need to live the life that you have been given.

You have your own dharma (purpose) in life.

You are not mature until you know how to control your emotions, know how to communicate properly, know that you don't have to wait for an apology to forgive someone, and accept accountability without blaming others.

Do no harm to anyone. Adopt the Passive Resistance Nonviolence philosophy of Gandhi & MLK. There is absolutely nothing that can be gained with violence that cannot be gained through dialogue and listening at a round-shaped table.

This is ***perspicacity***.

Be Well and please write to me and let me know how this book helped you gain the ***wisdom to know the difference***.

~Sujata~

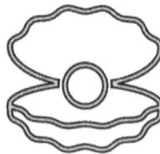

Dr. Sujata Ives, PhD, CCC, GCDFI, OWDSI

Dr. Sujata is a professional speaker with a distinctive voice! She truly is the work, life, and success Guru, and leaves audiences wanting more!

She is an accomplished leader and workplace global consultant in the field of career development, workforce analytics, and human flourishing. She is a sought-after national and international speaker that has published two books. "Activate Success – Tips, tools, & insights to be a Leader in Your Niche" made the international best-selling status on Amazon and Kindle. There is a Workbook by the same title. Her second book is this one!

Sujata is the 2023 recipient of the National Career Development Association's (NCDA) Diversity Initiative Award. She was chosen to participate in the 2024 NCDA Leadership Academy class, where she conducted a study through a needs analysis on intercultural leadership. It was her positive experience inside the Leadership Academy that encouraged her to write her first book, and now that she has had experience as the Chair of the Leadership Academy in 2025, she felt confident in writing her second book!

As a military spouse, she has collaborated with leaders through her nineteen lifetime moves that gave her the opportunity to help multi-million-dollar systems. She leverages global talent to hold candid conversations regarding peacebuilding. In this vein, she was the 2023 recipient of the title "Global Visionary" given to her by the 6th Congress, OtroMundo, Colombia, South America.

Sujata is the Chair of the Leadership Academy of the NCDA; the Chair of the Program Committee of the APCDA; Community Coordinator of the World Council on Global & Intercultural Competency, UNESCO. She promotes Interculturalism as the next viable option to value humans and cultures.

Sujata is past president of the Maryland Career Development Association, past chair of the International Committee of the American Counseling Association. And treasurer for the Maryland Counseling Association.

Sujata has an earned Ph.D. in Educational Psychology and is a Harvard trained Mediator. She believes in autonomy to change, evolving and adapting career development in revolutionary times, creative resiliency, and applying knowledge to make this world a better place to work and live within the human ecosystem.

She has a limited private practice and can be reached at
www.drsujataives.com

Dr. Sujata Ives, PhD, CCC, GCDFI, OWDSI
Amazon Book: "Activate Success: Tips, Tools, & Insights to be a Leader in Your Niche"
www.drsujataives.com
info@drsujataives.com
LinkedIn: Linkedin.com/in/drsujataivesphd

About the Publisher

Becky Norwood is CEO of Spotlight Publishing House and is passionate about helping people turn their knowledge, experience, and ideas into meaningful non-fiction books.

As a Publisher, our team does not just focus on getting books printed—we focus on supporting our authors to make an impact. Whether you're an expert, entrepreneur, coach, or storyteller, we are here to guide authors through every step of the journey: from idea to outline, from draft to publication and beyond.

What drives us is seeing authors step into their voice and use their book to open new doors—whether that's launching a business, growing a platform, or changing someone's life with their words.

Your story matters. Your voice counts. And your book could be exactly what someone out there needs.

Find Becky Norwood on LinkedIn:
https://www.linkedin.com/in/beckybnorwood/
https://www.facebook.com/SpotlightBookPublishing
https://spotlightpublishinghouse.com

About the Editor

Dr. Jeannine Bennett holds a Ph.D. in Organization and Management and an M.B.A. in E-Business.

She empowers individuals and organizations to achieve their goals through her work as an entrepreneur, published author, professor, and professional editor.

For over three decades, Dr. Bennett has aided thousands in professional and personal success through expertise in e-business, strategic communication, change management, career strategy, and academia.

She established Vision to Purpose, a company offering career services, business consulting, and writing assistance.

Find Dr. Bennett on LinkedIn: www.linkedin.com/in/jbennettphd

Before you go can I ask you for a quick favor?

Good! I knew I could count on you! 😊

Would you please leave my book a review on Amazon?

Reviews are very important for authors as they help us sell more books. This will in turn enable me to write more books for you!

Please take a quick minute to go to Amazon and leave this book an honest review. I promise it doesn't take very long, but it can help this book reach more readers like you.

Thank you for reading,
and thank you so much for being part of my journey!

Here is the link:
https://amazon.com/review/create-review/?asin=

You can also leave a star rating only if you are crazy busy!

Dr. Sujata is a member of the
National Speakers Association and is
available to speak in your company!

Book her at:
https://calendar.app.google/esC7v9AkVC7EjPLN6

www.ingramcontent.com/pod-product-compliance
Lightning Source LLC
Chambersburg PA
CBHW042247040426
42335CB00043B/2868